Your Body, God's Temple

Biblical Principles for a Healthier Life

Ronald L. Kleyn, M.D.

Cover art and exercise illustrations
by Ramsés Noriega

Your Body God's Temple

Biblical Principles for a Healthier Life

Ronald L. Kleyn, M.D.

Essence
PUBLISHING

Belleville, Ontario, Canada

Your Body, God's Temple
Copyright © 2000, Ronald L. Kleyn

All Rights Reserved. No part of this publication may be reproduced, stored in a retrieval system or transmitted in any form or by any means – electronic, mechanical, photocopy, recording or any other – except for brief quotations in printed reviews, without the prior permission of the author.

All Scripture quotations, unless otherwise specified, are taken from the *New International Version* of the Bible (Copyright © 1973, 1978, 1984 International Bible Society. Used by permission of Zondervan Bible Publishers.)

Other versions cited include the *King James Version* of the Bible (Copyright © 1977, 1984, Thomas Nelson Inc., Publishers); the *New King James Version* of the Bible (Copyright © 1979, 1980, 1982, Thomas Nelson Inc., Publishers); the *Revised Standard Version* (Copyright © 1952, Thomas Nelson & Sons, Limited); *The Amplified Bible,* Old Testament (Copyright © 1965, 1987 by the Zondervan Corporation); *The Amplified New Testament* (Copyright © 1954, 1958, 1987 by The Lockman Foundation. Used by Permission); and *The Message* (Copyright © by Eugene H. Peterson, 1993, 1994, 1995. Used by permission of NavPress Publishing Group).

ISBN: 1-55306-054-7

Essence Publishing is a Christian Book Publisher dedicated to furthering the work of Christ through the written word. For more information, contact: 44 Moira Street West, Belleville, Ontario, Canada K8P 1S3. Phone: 1-800-238-6376. Fax: (613) 962-3055.
E-mail: info@essence.on.ca
Internet: www.essence.on.ca

Printed in Canada
by
Essence
PUBLISHING

To Katie, Zach and Sarah

WARNING: The information in this book is based on biblical teaching and is intended to improve your overall health. However, if you are on medication or under a physician's care for a chronic disease, be cautious about dramatic lifestyle changes. Specifically, it is recommended that you do not change your diet, exercise level, or institute a fasting program unless it is approved by your health professional. The prescription and herbal medications mentioned in this book should not be used as treatment for any medical condition unless directed by a physician and should be avoided by pregnant or nursing mothers.

TABLE OF CONTENTS

Acknowledgments 9
Introduction 11
   1. The Healing Power of Rest 23
   2. Finding Peace in an Unpeaceful World 49
   3. A Biblical Guide to Healthy Eating 79
   4. A Fast Track to Health – Exercise 113
   5. The Blessings of Self-Control 137
   6. Keeping in Touch. 163
   7. Learn to Celebrate. 187
Summary: Getting Started on Temple Maintenance . . 209
Appendix 1: God's Attributes 225
Appendix 2: Who Am I? 229
Endnotes 233

ACKNOWLEDGMENTS

Many special people helped make this book possible and I want to extend my gratitude:

First, to my wife and children. Not only did I receive from my family encouragement, space and time to research and write, but each contributed individually: Katie gave invaluable editing advice and input – making sure the book resounded with grace; Zach helped with computer graphics; and Sarah gave assistance related to the artwork.

My brother-in-law, Ron Morris, has challenged me and laid down his life consistently for many years in interceding for my family and this project.

When I asked Ramsés Noriega to do the line drawings for the exercise chapter, I didn't realize I was receiving the services of an internationally known artist. Having him do the cover art was also a great blessing.

This project began with my taking a ten-month sabbatical in 1995. Many thanks to Drs. Patrick Stuart, Bob Graham, Ken O'Brien and Mary Sadlek for allowing me to take off, and for their gracious covering of my practice, along with Dr. Richard Blanks. Dianne Howes, the rest of the staff of Fresno Family Practice and many patients also deserve thanks for their encouragement and sacrifice.

Many people have been involved through prayer, and emotional and financial support. Some of these include Doug James, Steve Bolduc, David Hornor, Larry Briney, Tony and Jackie Miramontes, Phil Hinton, Dan Borgstadt, Ed Graveline, Bob Boyd, Frank and Diane Kessler, Gordon Ogden, Frank Rees, Linda Avery, Marilyn Totten, Ken and Sheri Fernandez, Mel and Sherry Hill, Richard and Marilyn Cunningham, Sister Tiziana Dalmassetto, Bob and Darlene Kleyn, my parents, Herb and Kathy Kleyn, and my in-laws, Bill and Vi Morris. Thanks also to my pastor, Brad Davis, at The Father's House, who allowed me to start the first "Temple" group study in the fall of 1999 and for the brave and delightful members of this "guinea pig" group. Howard Dayton, of Crown Ministries, has also provided much needed advise and support.

Dwaine and Jeanie Rose not only provided encouragement and prayer, but allowed me to stay with them at the Emmaus House, where I did most of my writing.

Scott and Sandi Tompkins spent many hours editing and partnering with me, turning a very rough draft into this coherent, organized form.

Willow Bouma and the rest of the staff at Essence Publishing have been outstanding in their assistance and flexibility with this project.

Most importantly, thanks goes to Jesus Christ who sustains, comforts and loves me. Glory to Him.

INTRODUCTION

Do you not know that your body is a temple of the Holy Spirit, who is in you, whom you have received from God? You are not your own; you were bought at a price. Therefore honor God with your body (1 Cor. 6:19-20).

As a family physician, I see hundreds of patients each year. They come hoping I'll cure their pains and diseases, but the medicines and treatments I prescribe – as potent and technically sophisticated as they may be – don't give patients the vibrant health they desire.

Treating their infections with antibiotics usually helps but does not seem to lessen the number of infections. Giving pills for hypertension, arthritis, heart disease, or diabetes sometimes controls symptoms, but it does not bring truly vigorous health to people, and it often causes unwanted side effects. The increasing costs of health care is also an issue.

Though most people with recurring infections or chronic diseases like hypertension or atherosclerosis tend to think their health problems are a combination of bad genes and bad luck, the truth is, these people are most often sick because of bad choices. Through ignorance, lack of self-control and faulty beliefs, people make bad choices every day that affect their health and gradually result in degeneration of the body.

The Bible is God's instruction manual for life. Most Christians see it as the source to find direction for their spiritual lives. Many have come to realize through Crown Ministries and the teachings of Larry Burkett and Ron Blue that God's Word also contains financial principles that, if followed, can bring us to financial freedom. Dr. James Dobson and his ministry, Focus on the Family, have provided people all around the globe with resources that teach about family relationships – all based on Scripture. Therefore, it should not surprise us too much that God's Word also contains physical health principles – principles that can lead the sick to recovery and keep the well in abundant health.

Just as the world's financial principles are at odds with what God says, so the world's health principles are often different from what God teaches us in His Word. Nevertheless, some of the world's research has supported the Bible's centuries-old precepts, and we will occasionally mention these studies as well. Unfortunately, these particular studies are often neglected. One of the most common reasons is that there is less profit to be found in these simple preventive truths than there is in using expensive tests and medications. I am not saying that most physicians are trying to gouge your wallet, but they have been trained and are part of a system that looks at health from a sickness model.

Why not change our perspective and look at health instead from a wellness model?

My personal interest in this model began when I was young. I grew up in a Christian home, the youngest son of a general surgeon. Early on, I was interested in the various ways that medicine dealt with health problems. But what fascinated me most was the design of the human body itself. I remember closing a pocket knife on my right index finger when I was about ten years old. My father repaired the cut with three stitches. Suddenly, I was struck by the fact that my body had the ability to heal and restore itself, and I wanted to know why.

I became interested in nutrition when I was in high school. It was a concept that made sense to me. Instead of dealing with the results of poor health habits, why not prevent them by eating properly? I was rather odd about my nutritional convictions, especially for a teenager. When I went with friends to Baskin-Robbins, they would order ice cream, and I would order a banana. Not a banana split, mind you, but just a lonely banana. Somehow, I did not mind the ridicule because of my intense desire to treat my body well. But the biggest challenges to my convictions were yet to come. During college I committed my life to Jesus Christ, and soon both my Christian faith and my beliefs about preventive care came under assault when the Lord directed me into a career in medicine.

Medical school offered little instruction on nutrition or preventive medicine. Instead it overwhelmed me with details on biochemical pathways, microbiology and pathology. My vision of a wellness model of prevention gave way to the disease model of modern American medicine. Meanwhile, the strongly humanist bent of my medical school lecturers challenged anyone coming from a Judeo-Christian worldview. There was little to no encouragement for a seeker of spiritual answers. And there were very few Christian role models among the professors and teaching physicians. If it had not been for some believing friends and especially our Saturday night worship times together, it is hard to imagine how my faith could have survived. Yet the Lord encouraged and directed me.

After being in practice for several years, and experiencing the frustration of making little headway in treating chronic diseases, I began again to consider the benefits of preventive medicine. The themes of preventive medicine and Biblical faith collided in 1994 when my wife Katie and I were taking a Crown Ministries class for the second time. As mentioned before, Crown teaches Biblical principles that lead to financial health. As I was going through these studies, the Lord was giving me a burning desire to see a similar study that would teach God's principles for physical health. If church members can benefit from applying what God says about money to their financial situations, surely they can also benefit from applying His truth about the care of their bodies.

Are God's People Healthier?

Is there any difference today between the health of Christians and that of non-Christians? Sadly, the answer is no. Should there be? I believe there should. I believe the church should be an example to those around that God desires His people to be healthy and whole, and that His Word holds truths which, when applied and lived out, restore health and prevent illness.

In Exodus 1, there is a brief story that supports this view. Pharaoh had instructed the Hebrew midwives to kill any boy infants but to let the girl infants live. The midwives disobeyed him. Their excuse: *Hebrew women are not like Egyptian women; they are vigorous and give birth before the midwives arrive* (Exod. 1:19). Now the midwives may have been lying to Pharaoh, but I believe there was truth in what they said. Their diet and lifestyle no doubt facilitated faster and easier labors. Later, in Exodus 15:26, God speaks to the people after they left Egypt, saying, *If you listen carefully to the voice of the Lord your God and do what is right in his eyes... I will not bring on you any of the diseases I brought on the Egyptians, for I am the Lord who heals you.* The message here is clear – obedience promotes good health.

Selfishness or Stewardship?

Before we go further, let's deal with the question of selfishness. Is it prudent to take excellent care of our bodies or is it selfish and self-centered? Is it sinful to neglect our bodies or should we attend to more important spiritual stuff first? After all, the Bible says that God does not look at outward appearances, but on the heart.

After the greatest commandment of loving God, Jesus said the second one is to *love your neighbor as yourself* (Matt. 19:19). The implication is that we already love ourselves. It is expected that we love and take care of ourselves. Loving self calls me to stewardship of my body – which models sanity and balance, which delays the onset of degenerative diseases, which lengthens my time of service, which frees up resources for more important things besides hospital bills and doctor visits.

There obviously needs to be a balance. Some people exercise so much they neglect their families. There is a threshold people can cross over from rest to laziness. Satan and his angels use both extremes. When we talk about self-control and food guidelines there can be a great temptation to become legalistic and forget about grace, mercy and love. None of these guidelines or principles are criteria for who is saved and who is not saved, who is more spiritual and who is less spiritual. We need to look at them individually and ask the Lord, "What would You want me to do with this? How are You leading?"

A few years ago the phrase "wounded healer" was widely used to describe those in the healing or helping professions who serve others with an empty cup. In one sense we are all "wounded healers" who need to be healed so we have something to give those around us. If I go to work with pneumonia, I am causing more problems than I am helping. If I work 60- to 80-hour weeks, abuse my body with excess coffee or sugar, and neglect proper rest and exercise, I may temporarily do more service for the Lord (or my business), but in a few months or years, there will be consequences. My body will simply wear out. That is why we need to live in balance. We must think about our long-range health goals. Good stewardship of our bodies will allow us to serve God without unnecessary sickness, pain or early death.

Our Model – God's Temple

Through Israel's early history, the Lord assured the people of His presence through clearly visible reminders – the cloud, the pillar of fire, the Tabernacle, Tent of Meeting, and the Ark of the Covenant. But when David was made king over Israel he felt guilty *living in a palace of cedar, while the ark of God remains in a tent* (2 Sam. 7:2). The Lord was pleased with David's desire to build a permanent dwelling place, but He revealed that it would be David's son Solomon, not the king himself, who would build this temple.

The description of the building process of that temple begins in 1 Kings 5. From its pages we see eight principles that were important to the design and construction process:

    1. It took time. At the end of 1 Kings 6, we see that it took seven years to build the temple. Quality work takes time, with intervals of quality rest.

2. **It was a peaceful process.** There is an interesting comment in 1 Kings 6:7, *In building the temple, only blocks dressed at the quarry were used, and no hammer, chisel or any other iron tool was heard at the temple site while it was being built.* The quiet at the building site created an atmosphere of peace.

3. **The finest materials were used.** There was no skimping on building the temple of God. Expense was not an issue. Cedars from Lebanon, olive wood and pine for doors, quality stone, burnished bronze and pure gold are some of the materials listed in the account. The use of cedar and gold speaks of something built to last.

4. **It took physical effort.** The temple was about 150 feet long, 75 feet wide and 45 feet high. Building this grand structure without power tools, cranes or electricity took a huge effort.

5. **It took community.** To compensate, they had a tremendous number of workers: 10,000 men each month went to Lebanon to work with the wood gathering; 70,000 men were assigned as carriers; 80,000 men were stonecutters; 3,300 were foremen.

6. **It took discipline.** With all the laborers involved in the building process, it took a fair number of supervisors to direct the project in an orderly manner. Without the discipline imposed by oversight and control, the work would have slowed down and the temple would not have been built as designed by God.

7. **There were dedication and celebration.** Once the temple was completed and the ark placed in the Most Holy Place, the Lord demonstrated His presence in the temple by filling it with a cloud. Solomon then offered a prayer of dedication followed by an enormous animal sacrifice – 22,000 cattle and 120,000 sheep and goats! They celebrated for two weeks. They went home joyful and glad in heart.

8. **There were conditions.** During the building process, the word of the Lord came to Solomon:

As for this temple you are building, if you follow my decrees, carry out my regulations and keep all my commands and obey them, I will fulfill through you the promise I gave to David your father. And I will live among the Israelites and will not abandon my people Israel (1 Kings 6:12-13).

This is an echo of Moses' words in Deuteronomy 30 where he states,

See, I set before you today life and prosperity, death and destruction. For I command you today to love the Lord your God, to walk in his ways, and to keep his commands... then you will live and increase, and the Lord your God will bless you.... But if your heart turns away and you are not obedient... I declare to you this day that you will certainly be destroyed.

The New Temple for God's Spirit

In the New Testament we read about another temple. It is still a temple of God. In fact, it is called the temple of the Holy Spirit. However, it is not a building in Jerusalem on Mt. Moriah. It is not a building at all. It is our body!

Isn't that incredible? God through his Holy Spirit has chosen not to dwell among us, but in us – in our physical bodies!

> *Do you not know that your body is a temple of the Holy Spirit, who is in you, whom you have received from God? You are not your own; you were bought at a price. Therefore honor God with your body* (1 Cor. 6:19-20).

After the temple was completed and the ark brought in, God filled the temple with the cloud of His Glory. When the body is knit together and God's Holy Spirit invited in, God's glory takes up residence. The human body has been the subject of centuries of art because it is both amazing and beautiful. God designed it, and it can reflect a degree of God's glory which can increase when God's Holy Spirit resides there.

The same principles Solomon used in the building of God's temple, I believe, can be used and applied to the building of God's Holy Spirit Temple – our bodies.

1. **It takes time with proper rest.** The seven years it took to build the temple is a parable on the Sabbath principle. We cannot neglect Sabbath and still have healthy physical temples.

2. **It can be peaceful.** Since God is the God of peace, He can show us how to deal with stress and anxiety and experience His peace despite our circumstances.

3. **It requires the finest ingredients.** The building materials for our physical bodies are the food, water and air we ingest every day. We need food that is health producing, that can build a strong, fit body.

4. **It requires physical effort.** The effort required correlates to our body's need for physical exercise. Though modern conveniences have made our lives easier, they have taken away the healthy strain on our heart and muscles that strenuous work demanded.

5. **It requires self-control.** Discipline is essential in the building of our body-temples. Through the Lord's strength we gain the ability to be self-controlled in lifestyle and habits.

6. **It requires community.** We can't do it alone. We need each other, we need relationships, we need closeness and we need human touch.

7. **It involves dedication and celebration.** As Solomon dedicated the temple to God, so we can dedicate our bodies as temples of the Holy Spirit, as living sacrifices. And we can celebrate – to laugh, to rejoice in the Lord.

8. **It requires maintenance.** Maintenance is the process of continuing to be faithful as a steward of God's temple.

So let's return to the temple Solomon built. What happened to it? After years of neglecting God's commands and principles (sometimes out of ignorance and sometimes out of rebellion), disaster eventually resulted. The temple was neglected, or desecrated, or defiled or ransacked. Defilement of the temple occurred from sinful acts in the temple. The people allowed things in the temple that should never have been: pagan religious practices, sexual immorality, idols. In 2 Chronicles 36, the writer describes the fall of Jerusalem when the Babylonians, under Nebuchadnezzar, carried away all the articles and treasures of the temple. Then they set fire to the temple. Why did they destroy the temple? It was the source of their spiritual life.

Today Nebuchadnezzar (Satan) carries away the articles and treasures of our temple (our body). Because of not following God's principles of health, our ability to fight off the invaders is weakened and disease and sickness occur. Many of us are living in temples that are ransacked, broken and neglected. The good news is that change can occur. Repair and rebuilding of the temple is possible.

After 70 years in captivity, a group of exiles from Babylon returned to Jerusalem to start the rebuilding process. Their first project was to rebuild the temple. But even before that, they rebuilt the altar. The altar was where they offered sacrifices. Before you start the rebuilding process of your physical health, offer your body to the Lord. Establish spiritual connections with the Lord first. Concentrate on your prayer life, your worship, your communion with the Lord. Then start the work of rebuilding the temple.

It may take a financial sacrifice. There will no doubt be opposition from without and within. There will be temptations and discouragement; at times it will feel like no progress is being made. But let a search be made in the royal archives (the Bible) to see if, in fact, the King (God) decrees that a rebuilding of this temple (your body) should be done. I believe you will find the decrees (the principles) as you read this book and study God's Word. And may God, who has caused His Name to dwell here (in our temple) overthrow any king or people (any distraction of the enemy) who lifts a hand to change this decree or to destroy this temple.[1]

After the temple was ransacked and burned, and the people carried off into Babylon, Scripture records an interesting footnote in 2 Chronicles 36:21: *The land enjoyed its Sabbath rests; all the time of its desolation it rested, until the seventy years were completed in fulfillment of the word of the Lord spoken by Jeremiah.*

The first step to recovery and rebuilding is rest. We will explore the topic of rest in the next chapter.

Ronald L. Kleyn, M.D.

CHAPTER ONE

The Healing Power of Rest

Who among us hasn't said, "I just need to get away," or "I'm not getting enough sleep," or "I gotta take a break." Stress and sleeplessness are reaching alarming levels nationwide with dire consequences to our health and quality of life. Yet despite the obvious need for Americans to get more and better rest, proven biblical principles of rest seem almost novel in our culture, even among Christians.

For most of us it's not a matter of having ample free time, it's a matter of choosing to rest. Everything in our fast-paced, success-driven, activity-filled culture seems to argue against it. We live with constant pressure, both internally and externally, to strive, to go, to get and to do. So naturally, we extend that pressure to our evenings, weekends and vacations. Slogans like "Just Do It" and "No Fear" feed this national state of drivenness by projecting the notion that we become winners by pushing our bodies to the limits of endurance. But the choice to live in the extremes, to push ourselves day after day without sufficient rest, always takes its toll. For many, it results in loss of health and premature death.

As a physician, I see consequences of insufficient rest etched in the faces and bodies of my patients every day. I feel great compassion for them because I, too, live with the pressure to push myself beyond healthful limits. Men and women whose decisions affect the health or safety of others typically feel an extraordinary amount of responsibility and stress, but that is all the more reason for us to get adequate rest. When we allow our work or activities to continually overtax us, the results are entirely predictable – poor or insufficient sleep, greater susceptibility to sickness, irritability toward those we live or work with and impaired judgment.

I believe rest is God's most important preventive health principle. Though I also believe strongly in the importance of eating the right kind of foods, exercising, avoiding destructive habits and other health principles, rest is the foundation of them all. God Himself modeled the principle of rest in the creation of our world. Genesis 2:2 says, *By the seventh day God had finished the work he had been doing; so on the seventh day he rested from all his work.* If our all-powerful God, who never grows weary, considered rest so important to our well-being that He instituted a regular period of rest for His people, then we would be wise to follow His lead.

Rest is the avenue through which God refreshes and restores us physically, giving our bodies time to heal and our spirits time to be renewed. Abraham Maslow, in his study on the hierarchy of human needs, places rest among the foundational physiological requirements of human existence along with food, air and water. When rest is missing, death occurs. When it is inadequate, sickness, psychological stress and confusion rule.

Balancing rest and work

My friend Doug's story illustrates the need for balancing work and rest. Doug was ordered to move his car repair business because of a change in city zoning laws. When the city's deadline came, he still hadn't found a suitable site, so he moved into a temporary facility. Working long hours in this damp and drafty, old building caused Doug to develop pneumonia and to lose nearly a month of work.

When Doug returned to work, he started taking weekends off. But because he was still struggling financially, he began doing evening work for a local utility company. Often he didn't get home until after midnight. He usually didn't see his children at all during the week. After continuing at this grueling pace for several months, he and his wife, Pam, decided the extra income wasn't worth it. Doug said to God, "I can't do this any more. I'm not going to work evenings or weekends. I plan to take yearly vacations with my young family. If this business is going to make it, it will have to be you." He began trusting God to supply what his family needed. To his amazement, his regular business began to grow steadily, and despite working fewer hours, his income increased progressively. He was also able to get six or seven hours sleep rather than the usual three or four.

Even people who should know better, lose their perspective on this. A few years ago, while I was talking to two other physicians, one began telling about a local physician who canceled his much-needed family vacation at the last minute to care for a patient who had become seriously ill. I was amazed that both fully supported this as the right decision. Pastors are another group driven by the needs of others. My wife and I visited a church once and heard the pastor's wife describing his lifestyle. She said he rarely took time off. He made it a policy to accept all dinner invitations from members and to be available night or day when they needed him. He did this despite the fact that he had several other full-time pastors on his staff. That kind of lifestyle is neither healthful nor consistent with Scripture.

Just as rest had its beginnings in the creation account, work was also initiated then by God. Work was not a curse. It was part of God's original plan. Adam was tending the garden before he ate the forbidden fruit. The introduction of sin, however, made work harder and allowed for two imbalances. The first, laziness, is described several places in Scripture. In Proverbs, Solomon praises the industriousness of ants and warns sluggards to heed their example. In 2 Thessalonians 3:10, Paul gives a simple rule that may seem callous to some, but if followed, would radically alter welfare as we know it. His rule: *If a man will not work, he shall not eat.*

> "No rest 'til the work's done, and the work's never done."
> —*Unknown*

The other extreme was demonstrated by Lazarus' sister Martha in Luke 10. She was drawn into the urgent and missed out on the important. Today we call that "workaholism." It can be defined as working so hard that other important parts of life are neglected. Those "other parts" might include our marriage, family, friends, personal health or our relationship with God.

While laziness seems obviously contemptible, workaholism is a subtle evil. Instead of labeling it as sin, we are tempted to view it as dedication or commitment. Because work was instituted by God, we sometimes jump to the conclusion that doing more will make us more blessed. Tim Hansel, author of *When I Relax I Feel Guilty*, writes,

Yes, work is both good and necessary. It should be pursued with diligence, honesty and pride. But it should not be worshipped and glorified as the basis of human dignity and worth. People are valuable totally apart from their job productivity. Work never saved anyone from sin, death or evil, nor has it unilaterally produced faith, hope and love. When work becomes a person's all-consuming interest, even if the work is good and necessary, it is idolatry.[2]

And as illustrated above, the church is often not the place to turn to for help in this area. What could be more important than spreading the gospel, teaching a Sunday school class or feeding the hungry? Well, how about listening to Jesus? How about sitting at His feet, ceasing from striving and receiving His love? When Christian workers equate full-time service with 24-hour-a-day availability and the responsibility to say yes to all requests for help, then they are setting themselves up for physical and emotional burnout.

True resting is, in essence, a type of work or discipline. It takes effort to say no. It takes effort to plan a day off, a weekend away or a long-needed vacation. There are so many good things that could be done right now. But God doesn't want us to settle for the good. *He wants us to choose the best.* And the best gift God gives us to balance work and play and to teach us rest is the Sabbath.

> "If I rest, I rust."
> —Martin Luther (on his life prior to his insight that "the just shall live by faith")

God's Rhythm of Rest – the Sabbath

Nearly 100 times, the Bible exhorts us to observe the weekly Sabbath day of rest. God modeled this principle at the Creation in Genesis 1 and instituted it as law in the Ten Commandments. He says,

> *Remember the Sabbath day by keeping it holy. Six days you shall labor and do all your work, but the seventh day is a Sabbath to the Lord your God. On it you shall not do any work, neither you, nor your son or daughter, nor your manservant or maidservant, nor your animals, nor the alien within your gates. For in six days the Lord made the heavens and the earth, the sea, and all that is in them, but he rested on the seventh day. Therefore the Lord blessed the Sabbath day and made it holy* (Exod. 20:8-11).

Does this ancient law still apply to modern man? And are we under any legal requirement to follow it? Yes and no. We are not bound by law in the same way Israel was, but because the Lord blessed the Sabbath, we are missing out on His blessing if we don't observe it. Let's look at some of the reasons for observing a weekly Sabbath rest:

- It is a time of refreshment (Exod. 23:12).
- It is a time for worship (Ezek. 46:3).
- It is a sign to the people that the Lord makes them holy (Exod. 31:12).

- It is a reminder that the Lord of Creation rested (Gen. 2:3).
- It can prevent calamity (Neh. 13:15-22).
- It can bring protection from the enemy (Jer. 17:19-27).
- It is a time for sacred assembly (Lev. 23:3).
- It brings blessings to the people who observe it (Isa. 56:2).

In her book *Keeping the Sabbath Wholly*, Marva J. Dawn says:

To keep the Sabbath holy means to recognize that the rhythm of six days of work and one day of ceasing work is written into the very core of our being. To observe that order week by week creates in us a wholeness that is possible only when we live in accordance with this pattern of being graciously commanded by God.[3]

In this context, regular observance of a day of rest is not a legalistic duty, but a way to find blessing and freedom. It is a time to cease not only our work, but our productive mentality, our anxiety and our attempts to be God.

Jesus repeatedly exposed and condemned the Pharisees' efforts to turn God's life-giving principle of rest into a form of bondage. In His life and ministry, Jesus reflected the Father's intent for the Sabbath as a time for mercy and instruction as well as rest. He set people free on the Sabbath (Luke 13:10-16). He healed on the Sabbath (John 5:1-11). He taught on the Sabbath (Mark 6:2). He declared that it was lawful to do good on the Sabbath (Matt. 12:1-14) And He pointed out to legalists of the day that *the Sabbath was made for man, not man for the Sabbath* (Mark 2:27).

> "Seven is the whole, complete number of God. When you take away Sabbath, you subtract one from seven, giving six, the number of Satan."
> —*Unknown*

We might wonder, then, writes Marva Dawn, about doctors and nurses, pastors and musicians, and other service practitioners who have to work on Sundays. On the one hand, we must avoid any sort of legalism about Sabbath keeping. Jesus himself healed on the Sabbath, and yet the Gospels strongly and frequently affirm that He faithfully observed the Sabbath. Preaching a sermon, playing an instrument for worship or in the symphony, or ministering to the sick might not be 'work' for some of us... On the other hand, some people will necessarily have to make their Sabbath another day besides Saturday or Sunday if it is to be a day without work. If such re-scheduling is necessary, the important thing is to make that day of ceasing from work a consistent habit, a regular rhythm of keeping the Sabbath every seven days... What God wants from us is a whole day that we set apart to honor Him by gathering with a sacred assembly and by ceasing from work.[4]

The Sabbath principle is one of trust. As we make one day holy to the Lord, neglecting our "to do" list and our agenda, we then truly entrust our time to Him. We can set aside our work, our labor, our loads (both physical and mental), and come and freely enter into the Lord's rest.

When we neglect the Sabbath rest, we may not be trusting the Lord to take care of us. We may say things like: "If I do not do this project on Sunday, it will not be done in time"; "It's my busy season, I have to work twice as hard now so I can rest later"; "I need to make all the money I can now because things don't look good for the future."

God has answers for these rationalizations. Philippians 4 says, *Do not be anxious about anything but... present your requests to God.* He knows our deadlines and limitations, and He wants us to declare by faith as Paul did, *I can do everything through him who gives me strength.* To those who claim they must work seven days during certain seasons, God says, *...even during the plowing season and harvest you must rest* (Exod. 34:21). To those who worry that there won't be enough for future needs, He reminds us of His care of the millions of Israelites wandering in the desert for 40 years. All through those years, God gave a double portion of manna on the sixth day so the people did not have to gather food on the Sabbath. He is the great provider.

The Sabbath principle corresponds with God's financial principle of tithing. When we give to God our tithe, the firstfruits of our labor and the minimum portion He requests, we are trusting Him to provide financially. The tithe of our time to God also shows our trust in Him. For many, this involves a weekly Sabbath rest and a daily time in God's presence. We then trust God to provide the time we need to do everything else.

A few years ago as I was conceiving the idea of a book on preventative health principles, the Lord directed me into a personal Bible study on rest. As this study was progressing and ideas began to surface, the Lord did an amazing thing. He provided the resources for me to learn firsthand about rest and Sabbath. A forgotten investment eight years before yielded an unexpected windfall. My wife, Katie, and I began to pray about what to do with the money. There were many options: reduce the mortgage on our house, give large amounts to charity, put aside some for our kids' education, take an extended vacation, etc. Then while talking to Katie and her brother, I mentioned I was about to start my seventh year with the same medical group. I asked for prayer about how to celebrate this sabbatical year. "That's what you should do!" exclaimed Katie. "Take some time off!"

About seven months later, our sabbatical began with a seven-week cross-country trip. The Lord had given the dream and worked out all the details. (It helped having understanding partners at work!) My ten months off not only included an extended vacation, they included an investment of time in my wife and children. In those ten months the Lord taught me about true rest.

One of the most inspiring passages on Sabbath rest says,

If you turn back your foot from the Sabbath, from doing your pleasure on my holy day, and call the Sabbath a delight and the holy day of the Lord honorable; if you honor it, not going your own ways, or seeking your own pleasure, or talking idly; then you shall take delight in the Lord, and I will make you ride upon the heights of the earth; I will feed you with the heritage of Jacob your father, for the mouth of the Lord has spoken (Isa. 58:13-14 RSV).

Couldn't each of us benefit from such blessing? Do you yearn for intimate fellowship with Him? Wouldn't it be wise to heed the instruction of the One who created our bodies and knows their needs for refreshment and healing? Absolutely! Sabbath rest is not only a doorway to intimacy with God. It's good medicine.

Learning to Be Still

Be still, and know that I am God, declares the Lord in Psalm 46:10. Our clamorous culture makes it hard to sit still, tune out the din and focus our hearts on God. Our own nature works against us in this. Learning to be still doesn't come any easier to us humans than it does to puppies, but it is a discipline worth learning. For us in western culture, the problem is even more pronounced. Concepts of reflection, meditation and contemplation are foreign to us, and this no doubt inhibits our ability to know God intimately. Even in our churches we seem hurried, with little time for quiet, listening, pondering, wondering.

> "The Lord is looking for people who will be still long enough for Him to rest upon."
> —*Tim Howard,
> Associate Pastor, Valley Christian Center*

Many of us are afraid of slowing down, afraid of silence. Perhaps we are afraid to just be and not do, afraid we will lose our identity when we cease our activity. If so, we can take encouragement from Mary who sat at Jesus' feet and listened, actively participating in the Lord's rest (Luke 10). Jesus honored her for this. We can also benefit by setting aside brief times to cease our strivings, quiet our anxious thoughts, turn off the television, and spend time with our God. For when we are lifted up in the arms of our Father, we begin to see things from His perspective and face life with eyes of faith, hope and clarity.

This reminds me of the San Joaquin Valley where I live.

The winters here are often blanketed by fog and everything seems cold and dreary. However, a short drive to the mountains takes us above this haze and allows clear visibility. Similarly, a retreat from the hectic pace of daily life allows us to get out of the fog of our routine and to see the big picture. We may begin to notice what's missing in our lives and to receive insight into what really is important and to receive vision concerning our current priorities and our future.

Practice just being in God's company with no agenda of your own. Allow yourself time to soak up His unconditional love. You may prefer listening to worshipful music as you wait in God's presence. You may wish to explore the discipline of contemplative prayer, learning to be comfortable with quiet. Books such as *The Practice of the Presence of God* by Brother Lawrence and *Open Mind, Open Heart* by Thomas Keating are great resources for this avenue to intimacy with God.[5]

Caroline Mayer, an excellent therapist in Fresno, has a simple recommendation for clients to learn "time out". She suggests setting a timer for five minutes, then sitting with good posture in a comfortable chair, feet flat on the floor, eyes closed, and palms down on the lap. Be aware of connections with the floor and your own body and notice and deepen your breathing. You may say a phrase which welcomes God to meet with you, or you may just concentrate on your breathing. This is a time to learn to "be" and to be with God, a time to learn to listen and not a time to think. When thoughts come along, imagine them floating away or flying off like a bird. Let them come and go without trying to control them. You will get better at this with time. End each session by pressing your heels on the floor to connect the relaxed state to a simple movement. Once you have a daily five minute meditation established in your schedule, consider adding one or two more. This is a wonderful way to feel almost like you've had a nap. This technique can even heal disturbed areas of the mind and help a person become internally cued by conscience and God.[6]

> "We have not given
> play and rest a proper dignity.
> We still have the conviction that
> the idle mind is the devil's workshop.
> We still have a subconscious guilt
> that if we enjoy life too much,
> something must be wrong."
> —*Tim Hansel,*
> *author of* When I Relax I Feel Guilty

Another great way to hear God is to occasionally take a personal retreat. I believe most of us would benefit greatly from taking at least two days away from home one to four times a year. Even if we live alone, getting away from our home and usual environment can be life-changing. It doesn't have to be expensive. Perhaps you have a relative with a beach or mountain cabin you could rent or borrow. The Catholic church often has retreat centers in large towns and in picturesque settings that are open to people of all denominations. Usually they are quite affordable. My wife and I have separately visited one such place about 2 1/2 hours from our home which accepts only donations. The times we have spent there have been monumental in our personal spiritual journeys. We have sometimes stayed in a motel, separately again, for our personal retreats. Ask the Lord to show you what you need here, and ask Him to provide.

Getting the Right Quantity and Quality of Sleep

Central to God's masterful design for renewing and refreshing the human body is sleep. Every living creature requires some form of sleep or dormancy. A typical human will sleep about 200,000 hours in a 72-year lifespan. Since we spend so much of our time sleeping (approximately one-third of our lives), we need to make sure our resting hours give us the refreshment we need for optimum vitality and healthfulness.

> "Sleep is God's contrivance for giving us the help He cannot get into us when we are awake."
> —*George MacDonald*

I believe the secret of good sleep is to get into a rhythmic, daily sleep pattern. Like the Sabbath, our sleep should follow a consistent cycle. The darkness of night reinforces this natural rhythm of rest. Because it is usually cooler and more quiet, nighttime is the period most conducive to sound sleep. Those who work nights disrupt this rhythm, but by sleeping at a consistent time, and darkening and quieting your rooms through shades, earplugs and other artificial means, you can achieve similar results. The most important thing is to determine how much sleep you need and set aside that time every day.

So how much sleep is enough? Physicians typically suggest we need six to eight hours of sleep daily to feel truly rested (more during periods of sickness or prolonged exhaustion). But Dr. Archibald Hart, author of *Adrenalin and Stress,* said this figure is based on research conducted with overstressed adults in urban settings. He contends that the average person needs eight to ten hours, and he suggests two methods to determine the right amount for you.

The first way is by gradually adding to your existing sleep period and monitoring the response. The second test requires that you be on vacation for at least two weeks. During the first week you may find yourself sleeping more because of prolonged weariness, but the second week's sleep pattern should give you a strong indication of your individual needs. Those who haven't been off for two consecutive weeks in the past five years should seek to schedule such a vacation. Many of us who have high stress jobs don't get completely rested until that second week. Sometimes we take vacations and don't rest at all. A whirlwind vacation in a place like Disney World can be wonderfully entertaining, but you may get less sleep than you do at home.

Some researchers disagree with Dr. Hart's conclusions. There have been studies that indicate people today are getting too much sleep, and that this is causing depression. My sense about this (based on patient histories) is that most of us get inadequate sleep. However, as we incorporate other healthful habits (like exercise and a good diet) the amount of sleep we need may diminish, and the quality increase. The main point here is to be open to the possibility that you may not be getting the right amount of sleep. Do some experimenting to find how much you need.

What about napping? Occasional sleep breaks can be quite helpful. I often make napping part of my Sabbath tradition. It helps me catch up on rest when I've had inadequate sleep during the week. A 15- to 30-minute nap can rejuvenate you for the rest of the day. I am less enthused about daily naps that exceed 30 minutes. These can interfere with your nighttime sleep patterns.

Sleep cycles and dreams

A somewhat simplistic description of sleep divides it into two separate phases. During non-REM (Rapid Eye Movements) sleep, which is the longer of the two, all body functions slow down and recuperate. In REM sleep, there are bursts of eye movement, elevation in pulse and blood pressure, and increased electrical activity in the brain. REM sleep is the phase when most dreaming occurs. During sleep, these two phases alternate. Typically, we experience 90 minutes of non-REM sleep, then five to 15 minutes of REM sleep. This cycle repeats itself throughout the night with some variation in the REM cycle (it tends to lengthen as one gets closer to waking).

We cannot enjoy sound sleep and still try to remain in charge of our unconscious time. In fact, one function of dreams is as a mechanism to reveal and work out conscious and unconscious feelings and struggles. Ecclesiastes 5:3 says, *A dream comes when there are many cares....*

Because dreams can give us insight from God, it is important to write down what we remember from them and pray about how to respond. God used dreams to warn Abimelech of impending danger in Genesis 20:3; to reassure Joseph about taking Mary as his wife in Matthew 1:20; and to encourage Gideon for battle in Judges 7:13-15. While they were slaves in foreign lands, a God-given ability to interpret dreams vaulted Joseph and Daniel into positions of great power and influence. There will be times when our dream's meaning will be obvious. Other times it will be a mystery but God will reveal it. Still others will remain a mystery, perhaps brought on by too much pizza or Aunt Freda's Mustard Custard.

A few years ago, I dreamed that I was at church with my two children and my wife Katie was at home. In the dream, there was an invitation to do a short-term mission in Africa, and we left immediately (only in dreams do you not have to go home and pack). When we got to Africa, I suddenly remembered I had not told Katie of our plans. The meaning of this dream was obvious to me – I needed to work on communicating with my wife.

Hindrances to Good Sleep

Our culture has found many ways to alter the body's natural rhythms, and we have paid for it through poor sleep and failing health. Caffeine and other stimulants turn us into rest-starved zombies; artificial lighting makes possible the swing and graveyard work shifts that flip-flop our body clocks; and the noise and other stimuli of all-night restaurants and entertainment spots drive us into sensory overload. This is not to bash progress, but to point out how we stress our bodies just by living with twentieth century technology.

Here are some factors that affect our sleeping patterns and ideas for how to correct them:

Environment – Many of us have trouble sleeping because of simple environmental things that can be easily changed. If your bedroom is too hot or too cold, invest in a fan, a warm comforter or whatever will solve your problem most economically. If your sleeping room is too noisy or too bright, try earplugs, eye covers, special room-darkening shades or heavier drapes. The noise of a fan can also drive out disturbing sounds that may be affecting your sleep. Lowering the lights in the evening triggers your brain to release melatonin, a body chemical that naturally prepares us for sleep.

The single most important environmental factor in your sleep may be your choice of a bed. Given the amount of time each person spends sleeping, a comfortable bed is one of the best investments we can make. Each of us will have personal preferences about firmness, but orthopedists generally agree that a mattress needs to be firm enough to give adequate back support. If you tend to have sleep problems, it would be wise to avoid reading, watching TV or eating in bed.

Factors associated with a new environment such as a new bed, new home or unfamiliar surroundings are also common causes of temporary sleeplessness. Jesus said to his disciples, *When you enter a house, first say, "Peace to this house"* (Luke 10:5). Many of us move into places without ever inviting the presence of the Holy Spirit. Ask God for His peace to descend on your new home or hotel room.

Sleep-inducing drugs – Sleeping pills themselves may sometimes be a cause of sleeplessness if used excessively, in wrong combination with other drugs, or without proper medical supervision. Prescription sleeping pills are usually sedatives (drugs that induce a calming or tranquilized state). When used over long periods, they may be addictive and disruptive to the body's natural rhythms. They should be used only with strict medical supervision.

Most nonprescription sleeping pills are antihistamines. We usually associate antihistamines with treatment of allergy and cold symptoms, but because they cause drowsiness, they are widely used in sleep medications as well. These are not addictive and are preferable to not sleeping, but ideally are not used daily.

There are two other over-the-counter products for sleep that I think are worth considering. Melatonin was mentioned earlier as a substance our brains produce in response to diminished light perception. Besides helping to regulate sleep, it is a powerful antioxidant. Be sure the brand you choose is not derived from animal sources. In this case, synthetic melatonin is safer. The second product is an herb called valerian root. It can be used for treating both anxiety and insomnia, and is sometimes combined in capsule form with melatonin. More research is needed on the long-term effects of these substances, but for short-term, occasional use, both are safe and effective for most people.*

Medical issues – Besides stress (which will be discussed below), several other medical conditions can cause sleepiness and fatigue. Temporary sleep difficulty may result from overexposure to the sun, low grade infections, pain, or breathing difficulty from colds or allergies. Hypothyroidism, anemia, cerebrovascular insufficiency, depression and sleep apnea can cause more chronic sleep problems. Consult your family doctor if you have one of these conditions, or if sleep problems persist after making environmental changes. He or she can help you determine the cause of your sleep problem and advise you on how to adjust your lifestyle or medication to assure adequate sleep.

> "He who cannot rest, cannot work; he who cannot let go, cannot hold on; he who cannot find footing, cannot go forward."
> —*Harry Emerson Fosdick*

The biggest hindrance to sleep – hyperarousal

In his book *Adrenalin and Stress*, Archibald Hart contends that there is a definite connection between excess

---

* Pregnant and nursing mothers should avoid these. Anyone on chronic medication or with a chronic illness should first check with their medical provider before taking.

adrenalin* in our system and the amount of stress in our lives, and that by controlling this "hyperarousal state" we can sleep better and reduce the damage caused by stress to our bodies.

The hyperarousal state occurs when adrenalin is pumped into the blood from the adrenal gland. This natural "flight or fight" response is the body's protective mechanism that alerts us to danger and sharpens our abilities in the face of an emergency. Wonderful as this God-given bodily mechanism is, it works against our ability to sleep. Almost everyone has experienced a loss of sleep at some time from adrenalin hyperarousal. For example, we typically have difficulty falling asleep on the night of an accident or some other crisis. We also may sleep fitfully on the night before an important event such as a wedding, a long-awaited vacation or an important business meeting. We lie awake thinking because our hyperaroused minds do not turn off. This is fairly normal when it occurs occasionally. However, if it is happening three or more nights a week, our health is being affected and help is needed.

The problem is that millions of us live in a constant state of being "hyperalert or aroused" because of stress from jobs, school, marriage, family or other pressures. I agree with Dr. Hart's view that this adrenalin overload is the most common cause of sleep disturbance today. The human body can live with stress for long periods, but eventually it will result in a loss of health. I strongly believe that God never intended us to live this way.

The Bible has much to say about this connection between stress and sleeplessness. Ecclesiastes 5:12b says, ...*the abun-*

---

* Hart uses the simpler spelling for adrenalin and I will maintain that here.

dance of a rich man permits him no sleep. Having many things just increases the worries and cares of this life. Simplifying our lives (by getting rid of stuff) may enrich our sleep. In Matthew 8:24-26, Jesus is able to sleep despite the raging storm surrounding Him. As we develop trust in God to protect and provide, we too learn to rest even in life's storms. We learn to release our cares and burdens, relinquish control and let go. Paul writes in Philippians 4:6-7,

> *Do not be anxious about anything, but in everything, by prayer and petition, with thanksgiving, present your requests to God. And the peace of God, which transcends all understanding, will guard your hearts and your minds in Christ Jesus.*

By casting our cares on Him, we can experience the peace that will bring us sleep.

God's Help for Good Sleep

God alone grants peace and security for good sleeping. Psalm 4:8 says, *I will lie down and sleep in peace, for you alone, O Lord, make me dwell in safety.* And Psalm 127:1-2 declares, *Unless the Lord watches over the city, the watchmen stand guard in vain. In vain you rise early and stay up late, toiling for food to eat – for he grants sleep to those he loves.*

Ecclesiastes 5:12a says, *The sleep of a laborer is sweet, whether he eats little or much....* The laborer, after working hard, is able to sleep well. When we don't do much manual labor, exercise can be a nice replacement. (We will be discussing exercise in a later chapter.)

The Bible also describes times or situations when we should be watching or praying instead of sleeping – the most famous being when the disciples couldn't stay awake while Jesus was agonizing in prayer at Gethsemene. There are times when sleep is not the priority, and we need to be keeping vigil with God. In Esther there is an example of how God can use times when we have difficulty sleeping to speak to us – sometimes without our even knowing it is God. King Xerxes couldn't sleep, so he thought having someone read to him from the chronicles of his reign might be just the ticket to take him to dreamland. However, he learned through his reading that Mordecai was never honored for saving his life. Through this incident Mordecai was rightfully honored, and saved from death, and it was the beginning of the downfall of Haman, the evil nobleman in Xerxes' court.

Perhaps the best sleep remedy of all is Scripture meditation. Psalm 1 describes the kind of man who is blessed by God, and verse two says, *His delight is in the law of the Lord, and on his law he meditates day and night.* When you can't sleep, begin reciting or meditating on favorite verses. This will draw your heart toward peace, and restful sleep may soon follow.

The Spiritual Connection – Rest for Our Souls

In Jewish law and culture, the Sabbath comes at the end of the week, after six days of work. In one sense, the old law is one of works and striving, and at the end comes relief and reward. In contrast, most Christians view Sunday as their Sabbath, their day of rest. Sunday, the first day of the week, comes at the beginning. Rest comes first, and prepares us for the remainder of the week. The New Testament is one of grace. We start in the sitting position as Watchman Nee describes in his book *Sit, Walk, Stand.* We begin in a position of rest, receiving fully His grace and salvation.

Jesus said, *Come to me, all you who are weary and burdened, and I will give you rest. Take my yoke upon you and learn from me, for I am gentle and humble in heart, and you will find rest for your souls* (Matt. 11:28-29).

God provides and instructs us about rest for our bodies; however, He specializes in showing us how to find rest for our souls. The beginning step is to respond to Jesus' compelling invitation to come closer to Him. As we do so, it becomes clearer that what are blocking us from having inner rest are the burdens we all carry. For everyone, this would include the mistakes and imperfections that make us human. The Bible calls these sins. For many, the burdens also include the emotional pain of past hurts and our response to them.

We enter this rest through faith – believing that Jesus is God's son and that He died for our sins (Hebrews 4). We exchange our crushing burdens for His easy yoke – releasing the heaviness of guilt and despair, and receiving the gift of holy fellowship with God Almighty!

We cannot earn this inner rest. It is not based on merit, good works or anything we could possibly do. It is a free gift for the asking – to those who come with believing hearts.

The Lord of the Sabbath invites us to experience the healing power of rest.

Let the weary come!

Practical Applications

Sabbath – The Jews called the day before the Sabbath, Preparation Day. I guess we call it TGIF. But the point is that a true day of rest does not come automatically. You need to prepare for it, plan for it and schedule it in. You may have to say, "No, I have plans for that day," to invitations you receive. Pray and ask God how He would want you to celebrate the Sabbath. It may be different each week. I find I often need time alone – to journal, to read, to catch up on sleep. You may enjoy and need relaxing fellowship, time outside or a drive to the country. Try to commit to a regular rhythm of weekly Sabbaths. But do not be legalistic. Remember the Sabbath was made to serve us.

Quiet time – This could be considered your daily Sabbath. Starting your day off with a holy connection with God establishes a restful pace to the day. It brings perspective and strength. Start with small time slots – 5 to 10 minutes, and increase as your hunger for God increases. Don't force it. Prayer, Bible reading, reflection and worship are some of the ways you can enjoy this time with the Father. Write down insights or impressions.

Retreat – Try to schedule a weekend away by yourself. No excuses. If you need it, God can provide for it. If married, help your spouse to schedule a personal retreat too.

Sleep – Consider the following when having trouble sleeping:

- Are there environmental things I can change that are keeping me from sleep? Is it too hot, too cold, too noisy? Do I tend to eat too close to bedtime?
- Determine your optimal length of sleep.
- Consider your inability to sleep as a way the Lord is speaking to you – inviting you to get up and read the Bible, or some other book, or spend time in prayer or reflection, or perhaps you need to write down what is troubling you.
- Keep a dream journal.

General Rest – Think back on the last time you were sick. Was lack of rest a factor? Could you have done anything differently? Could you have increased your rest to help speed your recovery? What are hindrances to your rest? Can you relax and be, or do you need to do?

Recommended Reading

Dawn, Marva J. *Making the Sabbath Wholly*. Grand Rapids: William B. Eerdmans Publishing Co., 1989.

Hansel, Tim. *When I Relax I Feel Guilty*. Chariot Family Publishers, 1984.

Hart, Dr. Archibald D. *Adrenalin and Stress*. Dallas: Word Publishing, 1986.

Lawrence, Brother. *The Practice of the Presence of God*. Nashville: Upper Room Publishing, 1950.

Keating, Thomas. *Open Mind, Open Heart*. Warwick: Amity House, 1986.

Mains, Karen Burton. *Making Sunday Special*. Waco: Word Books, 1987.

CHAPTER TWO

Finding Peace in an Unpeaceful World

Nothing rejuvenates me faster than a day at the beach. Watching the waves rhythmically advance toward the shore; walking barefoot in the soft sand; smelling the fresh, salty breeze; listening to squawks of soaring gulls and skittering sandpipers – all these join together to beckon my senses toward tranquillity and speak of God's infinite power, beauty and peace.

My daily life, however, seems far away from this peaceful shoreline. I navigate through rush-hour traffic to get to my office. There I am bombarded with people complaining of illnesses ranging from common colds to cancer. At home, though usually a place of refuge, there are the typical stresses that are part of a marriage and living with two teenage children. And if I watch the news (I usually don't), the day's breaking news brings anything but calm.

More than any infectious disease, we are all being exposed to an epidemic of stress in this country. Harvard Medical School associate professor Dr. Herbert Benson estimates that 60 to 90 percent of doctor visits today are for stress-related illnesses.[7] For some physicians this is a shocking disappointment. They chose their specialty over psychiatry so they could avoid dealing with "mental illness," and concentrate on "physical ailments." But as Dr. Archibald Hart describes, *...though stress begins in the mind, it ends in the body.*[8]

> "'tis the mind that makes the body rich."
> —*William Shakespeare*

The physical manifestations of stress can be unbelievably diverse, yet as real as a laceration and often more painful. Stress and anxiety can cause trembling – such as seen in someone with unsteady hands, a nervous tic or tremor. It can also cause the well-known symptoms of stagefright – butterflies in the stomach, dry mouth, cold hands, and rapid pulse.

But it doesn't stop there. Stress can be associated with a myriad of other symptoms including headaches, neck pain, back pain, chest pain, difficulty breathing, heart palpitations, abdominal pain, bowel disorders, cough, frequent urination, insomnia, infertility, etc. Terms such as "tension headaches," "irritable bowel syndrome," "hyperventilation" and "globus hystericus" describe physical disorders that are largely due to mental stress. And we are all susceptible.

A few years ago I developed a pain near my right shoulder blade. Initially I attributed it to either a pulled muscle or irregular sleep posture and expected it to quickly resolve. But it didn't. As I examined what else was happening in my life at the time, it soon became obvious that it was stress related. Against my better judgment, I had overcommitted myself by agreeing to mentor a physician-assistant student. Just recognizing the problem eased some of the tension. When I backed out of the mentoring commitment, my stress (and the shoulder pain) decreased further. Then, one Sunday morning at church, people were invited to stand if they needed healing for physical conditions such as back pain. Soon after they prayed for me, my back pain was completely gone.

In this case, the Lord used three channels to heal my back – insight into its relation to stress, removing myself from the source of stress, and healing prayer. One hindrance to finding peace is being closed to the idea that a physical problem has a psychological basis. There still seems to be a stigma attached to diagnoses related to mental illness. I have struggled with this myself. When my wife went through post-partum depression, I felt both embarrassed and helpless. We needed help, but I didn't want to talk about it. I have since come to believe that bringing things to the light – sharing it with those who love you and professionals who can help – gives the only hope for long-term healing.

When my patients come in with back pain, headaches or diarrhea, and the exam and work-up all point to psychological stress, it's sometimes difficult to get them to accept it. They would rather point the finger at structural problems, a family history or an intestinal parasite. While it is a mistake to assume all health problems are stress-induced, it is a bigger mistake not to look at stress as a major contributor to a large number of common ailments.

When we open up to how stress might be affecting our lives – then God can show us pathways toward peace and healing.

The Stuff Stress is Made Of

A study by Drs. Jonathan C. Smith and Jeffrey M. Seidel of Roosevelt University investigated the symptoms of stress in more than 1,200 subjects. In their published report, they said the most common symptom of stress was gastric distress. It was reported four times more frequently than the next highest symptom.[9] At first reading, I found this statistic somewhat surprising. I would have guessed headaches or back pain were more prevalent, though I see many stress-related gastric problems in my patients. In the King James Version of the Bible, the word *bowels* seems to indicate that our gastrointestinal tract is at the very seat of our emotions. The prophet Jeremiah cries out, *Behold, O Lord; for I am in distress: my bowels are troubled* (Lam. 1:20). And again, *My bowels, my bowels! I am pained at my very heart* (Jer. 4:19).

Other verses in the KJV, as well as later translations, also link the bowels with strong emotions. They use terms like "boiled, churned, anguish, distress, tormented within, and troubled" to depict negative emotions causing disturbance in the intestines. Conversely, other verses show strong positive emotions like compassion, yearning, affection, and even sexual excitement (Song of Solomon 5:4 KJV) affecting the bowels.

Life is a roller coaster ride of emotional ups and downs, and when we try to stuff these feelings, we lose our inner peace and head straight into physical trouble. It may be gastric distress. It may be diarrhea. It may be irritable bowel syndrome. It may be one of the non-bowel symptoms like headache or chest pain. Eventually, neglecting our feelings will bring harm to our bodies.

> "Worry does not empty tomorrow of its sorrow; it empties today of its strength."
> —*Corrie ten Boom*

One medical authority believes that all chronic back pain is related to unresolved mental stress that has been redirected. I don't completely agree, but if you are suffering from a chronic condition (especially headaches, back pain and gastrointestinal distress), you need to ask yourself if you are stuffing any emotions that might be the root cause of it. Then try to "unstuff" them with the treatment suggestions that follow. These will help put your body and mind at peace.

Recipes for Un-stuffing

Exercise – When we have stuffed emotions, we are like a spring under tension. One excellent mechanism to relieve that tension is physical exercise. A state of distress and anxiety includes excess adrenalin. Exercise provides an outstanding outlet for that adrenalin. It not only helps reduce the harmful effects of adrenalin, but also produces the positive endorphins that can reduce pain and give a greater sense of well-being.

I have found exercise is also a great way to release unresolved anger. When my anger is caused by a person (particularly a family member or close friend), I try to resolve it quickly by sharing my feelings with them. But sometimes anger stems from situations over which we have no control – like unreasonable requests, injustices, accumulated irritations or people we can't confront for some reason. Then what do we do? The anger still needs to be released.

A few years ago, I was given a punching bag for my birthday. I discovered that if I worked out with the punching bag whenever I came home feeling angry, most of the stress was alleviated. Sometimes as I was punching the bag I would shout things like, "I hate this heavy workload!" or "I'm angry, God, that I don't get enough time with my family." Sometimes I just made nonsense noise – grunts, groans, and screams.*

This is an example of what Paul meant when he wrote in Ephesians 4:26, 27, 31 about dealing with anger. I was releasing my anger, not holding on to it so it could damage my body, but being honest about the feelings. I was doing it through a healthy outlet instead of a destructive outlet like redirecting my anger at my patients, wife and kids or the family dog.

Confess your sin – Confession is good for the body as well as the soul. Through it, we gain peace with God and one another. David said in Psalm 32 that when he kept silent and did not confess his sins, his *bones wasted away*. In the same psalm, he describes the man whose sin the Lord does not count against him as being blessed. Confession and forgiveness are closely linked.

Confession is not just for sins such as adultery, theft, murder and drunkenness. Many people don't identify with those sins but, in fact, were the victims of such. The danger in this case is bitterness. As damaging as physical, sexual or emotional abuse can be, the key to healing for most victims is in their response to the evil done to them. Dealing with the bitterness and unforgiveness, confessing and letting go, can often cause a breakthrough in emotional and physical healing. This is not something that can be rushed for most victims. Forgive-

---

* Research indicates that for some people ventilation can cause an escalation of anger to rage and do little to dispel it. If you do this type of anger work, notice whether you are able to turn loose of your anger (the goal) or if it is making you feel more angry.

ness for them is a process that only God can bring to conclusion. Painful events must be seen and accepted before they can be released fully. A crucial part of this journey includes supportive friends and counselors as mentioned below.

Keep a journal – What a blessing that we have the book of Psalms in which King David exposes his innermost feelings and thoughts. They show his honesty with God as he shares not only his praises but his doubts and fears. They show his struggles with people as he vents his frustration and anger.

Many times we can release thoughts and feelings on paper that we are not ready to express out loud. Just the process of writing can trigger insights and bring clarity to a situation. And, because we tend to forget, recording a spiritual journal can be a way to help us remember what the Lord has taken us through. It also can be a wonderful heritage to future generations.

Find friendship and counsel – When we have a close friend or two with whom we can share our deepest feelings and emotions, we have a great gift. Having someone who will listen, encourage and, when necessary, confront, is a great blessing in helping us find peace. Friendships like this take time and effort to develop. (We will discuss this in greater detail in chapter 6.)

Sometimes in addition to a close friend, especially if emotional needs are overwhelming, a counselor is needed. This may be a pastor, a social worker, a marriage and family counselor, a psychologist or a psychiatrist. It may be someone in your church or other organization who has special skills or gifts in counseling others. Your physician or pastor may be able to direct you to the right person. Make prayer part of the seeking process. In general, finding someone who shares your faith and respects your value system would be the best choice. However, don't limit God. He can use non-Christians to speak to you and help you.

Some people avoid counseling because they are duped by the old stereotype that "anyone who needs this kind of help must be crazy." In reality, those who seek help may be the sanest ones around. Others shy away from counseling because they see it as uncovering old wounds that are painful. If a wound is painful, it means it has not been dealt with adequately. There is still infection that needs to be removed. Yes, it might be painful for awhile, but true healing can only come when infected wounds are opened and adequately cleaned. Love yourself enough to do this difficult work. There is no quick fix here.*

Find other outlets – What do you enjoy doing? Do you have a hobby, a musical gift or enjoy playing a sport? David was a musician. He played the harp to the glory of God. The Bible says that as David played, it soothed the emotions of troubled King Saul. I'm sure it was a source of comfort to David as well. We all need an outlet – a hobby, interest or escape which we can pursue to the glory of God. Music is a wonderful outlet, either as a participant for those with musical gifts, or as a listener. The type of music we listen to can have a profound influence on our nervous system. It can either excite or relax. Studies have shown that certain types of classical music can relieve tension and help children perform better in school.

I wrote most of this book at a retreat center in the foothills of California. On one occasion while I was there, the center was also hosting a small group of women who are survivors

---

* There have been more and more reports of dramatic emotional healing as believers begin to rest and wait in the presence of the Lord. I rejoice for this (after all, the Holy Spirit is the greatest Counselor), and would encourage people to pursue this while simultaneously pursuing a course with a gifted counselor.

of abuse. A couple of miraculous unstuffings occurred during our weekend together. One woman who had not played the flute for eight years picked it up and played during a time of worship. Another woman who had not sung for 20 years sang a beautiful solo. Buried gifts were being uncovered, and emotions were being healed. When we stuff negative emotions, we also unwittingly stuff positive emotions, gifts and talents.

Learn to relax – The Bible makes a strong connection between breath and peace. After Jesus was resurrected He appeared to His disciples in the upper room and said, *"Peace be with you! As the Father has sent me, I am sending you." And with that he breathed on them and said, "Receive the Holy Spirit"* (John 20:21-22). Earlier, Jesus told them He would be sending the Counselor, the Holy Spirit, and that *my peace I give you.* The Greek word for spirit is *pneuma*, which translates air or breath. This further confirms the connection between breathing, God's Spirit, and peace.

One exercise in tying these concepts together is to practice conscious breathing. It can be as simple as just taking a few deep breaths. You might want to imagine Jesus breathing on you (giving you spiritual CPR), giving you His Spirit and His peace as you inhale. As you exhale imagine yourself releasing the cares and burdens and stuffed emotions that have been lying deep within you. Continue this cycle for four or five breaths.

One further step in this relaxation exercise is to hold your breath for a count of seven after you inhale. Then exhale through the mouth taking longer to exhale than you did to inhale. By doing this you are pushing more air out of the lungs, which makes more room for air and oxygen to fill the lungs. If you do this on a regular basis, perhaps combining it with meditation, it will help bring peace to your mind and body. (See also chapter one for a five minute meditation).

Learn to laugh – Sometimes when we have stuffed emotions, we become stuffy and forget how to laugh. Lighthearted laughter can do wonders in lifting stress and bringing peace. We will address this topic more fully in chapter seven.

Fear – An Enemy of Peace and Good Health

One common source of stress-induced illness is fear. One day our family was playing a word game called *Balderdash*, and the word *agyiophobia* came up. Each of us made up a definition which was read aloud along with the real definition.

The object of the game is to fool others into voting for your created definition. The real definition of agyiophobia is the fear of crossing busy streets, but I liked the one that my son Zachary came up with: the fear of exploding toilets. His definition may seem absurd, but we humans can develop a dread of anything and everything – from darkness to spiders to computers. Many can be traced to a bad childhood memory or life experience. Others seem to have no rational basis, but can be equally debilitating.

> "Cast all your anxiety on him because he cares for you."
> —*1 Peter 5:7*

Richard Swenson, M.D., in his book, *Margin: Restoring Emotional, Physical, Financial, and Time Reserves to Overloaded Lives*, states: *Some researchers believe fear to be the root cause of all stress reaction.*[10] Because fears are such a common cause of anxiety-related ailments, let's look at some of the more prevalent ones. I believe that addressing these fear issues is a crucial step to finding God's peace.

The different faces of fear

A healthy fear of dangerous situations is a protection for us. This fear keeps us from putting our hand in a fire, jumping off tall buildings or exposing ourselves to emotional or physical abuse. It is a healthy fear that helps us slow down and assess a situation or seek guidance before we act.

When we become obsessed with the possibility of danger despite unlikely circumstances, however, we bring a danger to our health. Consider this extreme example from the early 1900s. Scientists at that time knew that Halley's comet would be returning in 1910 as it had done every 76 years since recorded history. However, they also predicted the comet would fly so close to the earth people would be exposed to a poisonous gas called cyanogen which might wipe out the entire human race. Because of this, unwarranted fear spread worldwide, causing many to seek shelter and some to commit suicide.

Living in fear, though not actual suicide, brings slow and subtle harm to our bodies. Some of these fears involve our own shortcomings. In the world of medicine there are not only fears of failure and lawsuits, but also paranoia that our humanness be found out. I once worked in an office where saying the word *oops* was strongly discouraged. In Matthew 25, the man who had only one talent hid his because he feared failure. Many people, out of fear of making mistakes, do not even try. We fear we will make a mess, so we don't even get out the ingredients. The kitchen stays clean and organized, but everyone is starving.

For people who had their feelings ridiculed, they may believe some emotions are "bad" and be afraid of showing or even admitting them. One of these emotions is fear;

hence the expression, "The only thing to fear is fear itself." As Christians, we may believe fear is a sign of unbelief, or that our fear, anger or despair is a sin. So we try to "be good" and pretend not to have these emotions. This is called "denial" or "lying to yourself," and can lead to self-righteousness and hypocrisy.

Living in fear can not only cause physical symptoms such as those mentioned earlier in this chapter but also spiritual paralysis. In the biblical story of David and Goliath, the whole Israelite army was so terrified of the Philistine giant that they couldn't move forward. The same can be true spiritually when our lives are gripped by fear. The bondage this brings to our spirits and bodies can be stifling. But there is hope – and a way to freedom and peace.

> "Fear is the place where love has not come yet."
> —Ron Morris

Dealing With Fears

At a men's retreat at Hume Lake Christian Camp a couple of years ago, I survived the "High Adventure" course. Despite my fear of heights and the possibility of falling to an untimely death, I signed up to participate in this faith experience, mostly because my teenage son had already signed up and this weekend was to be a father-son bonding time. We were two of the first in line for the most popular "exercise" – jumping off a 42 foot platform in a harness connected to ropes that a stranger controlled from the distant ground below. Just writing about the experience reawakens the fear I had at the time. But remembering the success I had in overcoming the fear also reawakens the lessons God taught me that day. Here they are:

Acknowledge your fears

Being on that platform 42 feet above the ground made me come face-to-face with my fear of death. There was no way to avoid it. I was like the alcoholic who had to admit his problem. Drs. Dan Allender and Tremper Longman, III, describe it this way: *If you avoid your fear, it will turn dark and destructive. Instead, allow it to stalk you without trying to wave it away by reciting pious platitudes or distracting yourself in busyness. Fear faced is a heart exposed.*[11] The answer to all feelings including fear is to experience them and let them pass through your body and be gone. It doesn't work to fight feelings!

It also helps to know you are not alone. Everyone who participated in the "High Adventure" course that day had to face his own fears. In fact, whenever anyone is in a situation that is unfamiliar, fear is bound to surface. Susan Jeffers writes, *The fear will never go away as long as I continue to grow.*[12] If we are growing, we will continually be experiencing new situations, and with those come feelings of fear we can acknowledge.

An additional step is to acknowledge fears to someone else. For example, years ago Katie and I went to the coast for a couple of days to celebrate our wedding anniversary. We hadn't gone away together since before Sarah's birth, five years before. That first evening I admitted I was afraid of how we would relate; this not only put Katie at ease, it opened the door to communication and a fun weekend. I believe this principle of discussing weaknesses is one reason we've been happily married 22 years. I encourage you to also bring up feelings – those closest to you will love you for it.

Wrestle with the fear

Standing on the platform watching my son and others jump off first gave me time to struggle with this fear issue. Is this fear warning me of a danger I should avoid or confront? What is behind this fear? Do I take flight (in this case, avoid the struggle and climb down) or do I fight (in this case fight was flight – literally)? God, how am I to deal with this fear?

Allender and Tremper describe this step:

> ...*we must struggle with our worry. This is in contrast to the philosophy that advocates 'simply trust Jesus and your worries will disappear.' Once you acknowledge your fears, you're in for a real battle. It's only after struggle that you will experience lasting peace* (see Psalm 131).[13]

Jesus is our prime example here as He struggled through His worst fears in the Garden of Gethsemene.

Consider God's perspective

At first glance it appears God's advice on fear is a short and simple, *Don't*. Looking more closely gives us deeper insights. In Isaiah 43:1-3, God says,

> *Fear not, for I have redeemed you; I have called you by name; you are mine. When you pass through the waters, I will be with you; and when you pass through the rivers, they will not sweep over you. When you walk through the fire, you will not be burned.... For I am the Lord, your God, the Holy One of Israel, your Savior.*

In other Scriptures, God, Jesus, angels and various patriarchs say essentially the same thing:

Do not be afraid *because of who the Lord is*.

Do not be afraid *because of what the Lord has done.*
Do not be afraid *because of what the Lord has promised.*

They are not saying to deny feelings, but rather when we find ourselves afraid, to not stay there. Instead, we can look to the One bigger than our fears and recall His attributes, His provision in the past, His promises for the future, and His power and willingness to meet us where we are. Admitting our fear and weakness can help us trust God and His answers and allow Him to be glorified.

On the platform that day, my choice was either to climb down (and avoid my fears temporarily) or to trust the ropes, harness and the man on the ground controlling my descent. Despite the appearance of danger, a safe jump to the ground occurred for me and everyone else that day.

A healthy fear of God is another key part in the process of recovery from anxiety. This is not to be confused with the fear Adam and Eve experienced in Genesis 3 when they ate the forbidden fruit and then hid from God. Cowering is an unhealthy fear of God, the kind of fear most world religions teach as the appropriate response to its deity. But this kind of fear is not Father God's intention in our relationship with Him. Yes, He is Almighty God. Yes, He is omnipotent, holy and righteous. Who He is instills in us great awe, respect, and fear. But instead of causing us to hide from Him, this holy fear beckons us to run toward Him and to live openly before Him.

Mark 10:32 reads, *They were on their way up to Jerusalem, with Jesus leading the way, and the disciples were astonished, while those who followed were afraid.* Following the Lord from a distance is dangerous and always adds an element of fear. Having a close relationship, on the other hand, creates astonishment – a sense of awe and wonder.[14]

> "A perfect faith would lift us absolutely above fear."
> —*George MacDonald*

A good way to start in developing this kind of relationship with God is by studying His attributes. Often we have a cloudy picture of who God really is. We may view God through the lens of our earthly father, and because no father is perfect, we connect those imperfections to our heavenly Father. When we begin to see clearly who God is, we learn He is someone we can fully trust. We develop a healthy fear of the Lord and our other fears and anxieties become smaller. The Psalmist says in Psalms 42:6, *When my soul is in the dumps, I rehearse everything I know of you* (The Message).

Getting to know the Lord is a lifelong pursuit worthy of our greatest efforts. Appendix 1 is a list of God's attributes and applicable verses. Consider reading over this list regularly or using the Scriptures as the basis for a personal study. But don't stop there. Talk with Him. Bask in His presence. Praise Him with song. Fall deeper in love with Him. As your love for God grows, fears begin to loosen and you begin to experience His perfect peace.

Step out in faith

Having trust in the equipment was solidified by my taking a step off the platform. Most often the last stage in overcoming a fear requires an action – asking for help, a crucial conversation, stepping out of your comfort zone. It won't be easy. You're likely to make some mistakes and learn from them. In Susan Jeffers words, *The only way to get rid of the fear of doing something is to go out and do it.* She also states powerfully, *Pushing through fear is less frightening than living with the underlying fear that comes from a feeling of helplessness.*[15]

As discussed earlier, knowing God lessens our fears. Walking with Him also at times requires a leap into the unknown. John Wimber used to say, *Faith is spelled R-I-S-K.* Another pastor says faith feels like jumping off the high dive into what looks like an empty swimming pool, trusting God to fill it before we hit. God honors this kind of faith and He'll be there to catch us and encourage us to jump again.

Expectations and Inner Peace

I was in a dilemma. During my sabbatical year – a time the Lord set aside for me to be with my family, to rest and to do some writing – the church we were attending announced that it would be participating in a medical missions trip to Nepal. They were looking for health-care professionals who could contribute their skills for this three-week mission. The most exciting news was that the doors of Nepal were opening wide for this group. After years of persecuting Christians and making laws forbidding evangelism, Nepal was actually inviting teams to come.

And here I was: a Christian physician who would be off work during this time, with skills needed in a ripe mission field. I felt heavy pressure as I struggled with this decision – not from my church leaders, but from within myself. As I was sharing my dilemma with one of my pastors, he asked me, "Well, what do you want to do?" His point was that God often shows us His will through our desires. He then prayed that I would be freed from others' expectations. He said, "Going because other people expect you to go is not the right reason."

What is it that compels us to take on expectations that become such heavy burdens? One factor is a faulty perception regarding abilities and needs. This could be stated in a mathematical equation: Ability + Need = Will of God. When there is a need and we have the ability to fulfill that need, we jump to the conclusion that it must be God's will for us to do so. It is not necessarily so. It may be God's will, but it may not be.

In John 5, Jesus visits the pool of Bethesda where a *great number* of disabled people are camped out in hopes of receiving a miraculous healing. Jesus singles out one invalid and heals him. It was a great miracle, but what about the others who were at the pool that day? Why didn't Jesus heal all of them? Surely he had the ability. I believe it was because He didn't allow himself to be driven by the expectations of others. In Mark 1:35-39 we see that Jesus, after healing many sick people one evening, retreated to a solitary place to pray. When the disciples found Him the next morning, they wanted Him to go back and heal more people. But Jesus said, *Let us go... to the nearby villages – so I can preach there also.* Certainly He could have stayed and healed more people, but He moved on because He knew that He had to follow God's timetable, not that of others.[16]

Treatment for Faulty Expectations

Trying to please others all the time is a certain set-up for stress and disappointment. No one can please everyone. No one can please even one person all the time. It takes wisdom, courage and perseverance to break out of the bondage of expectations. Below are some steps that will help us move into the peace and freedom that God intends for His children.

> "A good theology is an indispensable prerequisite to a good psychology."
> —*Neil Anderson*

Know your spiritual identity – Just as knowing God can help overcome fear, knowing yourself can help overcome faulty expectations. We need to understand our spiritual identity, our personality, and our unique stress symptoms.

Neil Anderson's book *Victory Over the Darkness* shows how we can overcome all kinds of anxieties and unrealistic expectations by simply living in the reality of our true identity in Christ. Appendix 2 gives a long list of positive confessions about our identity that come directly from Scripture. Speak them out loud. Read through all of them everyday or read a new one each day for a month. They will give you courage to live as a beloved son or daughter of the King of Kings.

Know your personality – I believe it is also helpful to get more specific in looking at ourselves as uniquely created beings. One way to do this is to look at our personality or temperament. There is danger in pigeonholing ourselves or other people into a man-made system, for we are all one-of-a-kind individuals. However, as a tool, these classification systems can bring insight to our lives and help lead us toward healing from anxieties related to faulty expectations.

The most common system separates the personalities into four basic types. These seem to be based on Hippocrates and his four humours (no joke) or bodily fluids: blood (sanguine), yellow bile (choler), black bile (melancholy), and mucous (phlegm). If this seems gross, it is. That's probably why people have taken those four fluids and renamed them with respectable colors, animals or titles.

Space does not allow me to go into great detail regarding this step. It will require that you do some reading and investigation of your own. Three of the more popular books on this subject from a Christian perspective are *Spirit-Controlled Temperament* and *Transformed Temperaments* by

Tim LaHaye and *Understanding Your Temperament* by Gary Smalley and Mike Trent. They also divide the personalities into four basic types, but give readers additional spiritual insights that instill a greater sense of peace about who God created us to be.

My favorite system divides the personalities into nine basic types. The types are given numbers one through nine and are illustrated through a nine-sided geometric figure. Hence, this system is called the "enneagram."[17] I prefer this system because I believe nine types instead of four gives greater accuracy. Plus, this system tends to deal with the "dark side" of our personalities. When our sin nature is addressed, amazing insight and personal growth can occur.

Know your unique stress symptoms – I believe it is helpful to identify where in the body we manifest stress. Each of us is unique, and we each have our areas in which stress shows itself through physical symptoms. Often it is through digestive tract distress, headaches, back pain or hypertension. Once we identify our stress symptom, we should next ask: How does it begin? How long does it last? What specifically is triggering this bodily response? Once the symptoms are identified, then you can step back and learn from your body. You begin to see what stresses you out. You begin to know what your fears are. And, as mentioned earlier, identifying the fear can be an important step to healing. Why? Because it is not in the dark anymore. This process involves learning from your mistakes, seeing the foe as a friend, allowing God to work through it and teach you.

Know your purpose – Why are you here? What is the primary focus of your life? Corporate America has learned the importance of composing mission statements for their businesses. These concise statements define the purpose of each particular company. It is what they can go back to when they need direction. It is the motivating force for them in going forward. It can be helpful to consider some of the mission statements in Scripture:

> John the Baptist: *A voice of one calling in the desert, 'Prepare the way for the Lord, make straight paths for him'* (Matt. 3:3).
>
> Jesus: *The Spirit of the Lord is on me, because he has anointed me to preach good news to the poor. He has sent me to proclaim freedom for the prisoners and recovery of sight for the blind, to release the oppressed, to proclaim the year of the Lord's favor* (Luke 4:18-19).

What about you and your life? Have you written a personal mission statement? If not, why not work on it? Here are some helpful questions to consider:

- Have I had a childhood dream that I have forgotten?
- What is God calling me to be and do?
- What are my greatest strengths?
- What am I passionate about?
- What is most important to me?
- If I had one year (or 5 years or 10 years) left in my life, what would I do?
- If I had unlimited time and resources, what would I do?

Play with these and other questions you come up with. Try to write something down on paper, without agonizing over this. Remember, this is to help relieve stress, not create it. Seek God in the process, and He will reveal your unique purpose in His time.

Set healthy boundaries – Recently, a patient told me of a remarkable success in redefining her boundaries. For the past 20 years, all of her children and their families (18 people in total) had come to her house for Thanksgiving dinner. She was expected to cook this meal without assistance from the family. This year she said, "No."

They countered with, "But we don't know how to cook, and you're such a great cook."

"No," she said firmly. "If you want to come and have dinner, then you'll have to take your father and I out to eat, because I'm not cooking this year." And that's what they did. Early on, those dinners were probably a source of joy and a wonderful gift to her family. Now they had become an enormous stress that took away from her enjoyment of her children and grandchildren.

No is such a small word, yet it seems so difficult for us to say. Certainly, it has not always been that way. Back when we were toddlers, most of us drove our mothers crazy with our incessant *No's*. We need to learn to start using that word again. When we know ourselves and our purpose, it becomes easier. For those of us who are people-pleasers, it might be advisable to not give a direct answer when we are asked to do something. Give yourself time to think and pray about your answer. If someone is pushing for an answer right away, then why not err on the side of saying *No*?

> "Simply let your 'Yes' be 'Yes,' and your 'No' be 'No'...."
>
> —*Jesus*

Evaluate your time management – We live in an age in which our lives tend to be fast-paced and a multitude of things are clamoring for attention. There does not seem to be enough time to go around. We learned from the chapter on rest, how important it is to break this frantic cycle and establish regular Sabbaths, retreats and healthy sleep patterns. So why am I now encouraging a time-management evaluation? Does this bring images of an endless to-do list, doing instead of being?

One key to balance is to adjust our thinking on time management. There have been major advances in the research and writing on this topic in the last ten years. The best time management tools first help us identify our values, then identify our life goals (personal mission statement), and then show us how to walk these out on a daily and weekly basis. These tools help us concentrate on those activities that point us toward our goals instead of running from crisis to crisis. When we know our purpose and goals, we can more easily say no to those things which are asked of us (often very good things), but are not part of our vision. This significantly reduces stress. We are not talking about rigidity and inflexibility. We are talking about a journey having a targeted destination. Time management tools provide a map which shows us how to get there and brings order to the process.

> "Teach us to number our days aright, that we may gain a heart of wisdom."
> —*Psalm 90:12*

The Stress of Overloaded Lives

Several years ago my wife confronted me about my schedule. I had allowed myself to get too busy with my work, spending more and more time at the office and away from my family. There were some good reasons – we were short-staffed at the office after one of the doctors had retired and we were still looking to replace him. I was doing some moonlighting because I felt we needed supplemental income. I was also doing some occasional charitable work in the Salvation Army clinic. When Katie confronted me, I could not see how the situation could change – at least not anytime soon. I felt locked in and out of control. You know how football teams get in as many plays as possible during the closing minutes of a game when they are behind. They do it without huddling. And it often works. But to go at that pace for prolonged periods of time can be disastrous. We need to stop and huddle.

That night while sitting alone on the couch I began to think about what Katie had said. I spent some time praying. I spent some time listening to God. Amazingly, within a couple of hours God had given me ten ideas on how I could change my situation so I could spend less time with work and more time with my family. And He gave me the grace to implement them. They were not easy decisions. It is not difficult to add things to life – a second job, a new responsibility at church, an expanded role in the office, volunteering at a child's school. But it is difficult to take things away. Once we start something, we feel inclined to finish.

And it is not just responsibilities that we add to our life. We live in a world where overstimulation is the norm. Our TV channels used to have three or four stations. Today, they have hundreds. Children in the past could sit down and enjoy a board game or puzzle. Today, they cannot sit still unless they're playing a video game or surfing on the Internet. If a family goes out to eat, it's often a fast-food restaurant that has a multimedia playland for kids and a large-screen TV for the parents. Rather than leading to a more fulfilled life, this sensory overload can lead to spiritual, physical and emotional bankruptcy (sometimes financial too).

Most of us cannot afford to keep up a relentless pursuit of material pleasures and possessions. But Israel's King Solomon was so rich that he let out all the stops. The Bible says he *owned more herds and flocks than anyone....* He amassed vast quantities of silver and had numerous wives and mistresses. He *became greater by far than anyone in Jerusalem* before him. Yet, was he satisfied? His words speak for themselves: *Yet when I surveyed all that my hands had done and what I had toiled to achieve, everything was meaningless, a chasing after the wind; nothing was gained under the sun* (Eccl. 2:11).

The only thing we gain from a full-on effort to satisfy material wants and satiate our senses are physical problems such as tension headaches, ulcers, tight muscles, gastritis, spastic colon, hypertension and the like. The computer phrase "garbage in – garbage out" applies here.

Treatment for "Too-Much" Syndrome

Simplify – After several months of living alone in the barren Arctic, Richard E. Byrd wrote in his journal, *I am learning... that a man can live profoundly without masses of things.* Hopefully, we can learn this principle without having to travel to the North Pole.

Jesus makes a connection between our anxiety and our preoccupation with things. After instructing us not to worry about our food, drink or clothes, He ends the discussion by revealing the central core in obtaining simplicity – seek His kingdom first (Matt. 6:25-33). There are other things we can do. One is to de-accumulate. Learn to give things away. Learn the secret of holding possessions lightly. Learn the secret of being content. Can we say with Paul, *If we have food and clothing, with these we shall be content* (1 Tim. 6:8 RSV)? Learn to live within your means. Assess your spending and set up a budget. Then ask God to help you follow it.

> "'Tis a gift to be simple, 'tis a gift to be free, 'tis a gift to come down where we ought to be...."
> —*Old Shaker hymn*

Find solitude – When we are overloaded with things and responsibilities, it is difficult to find peace until we can get away to a quiet place and evaluate our lives. This might be a personal retreat which we described in the first chapter.

However, try to find snatches of solitude during your normal days. This may be early in the morning before the family wakes up or a quiet moment outside before you go to bed. I usually try to take my lunch hour in my office at work and close my door. I have just spent four hours with people and have recognized that I need a moment of solitude before I face the responsibilities of the afternoon.

Meditate – Closely tied with solitude is meditation. We have already discussed a five-minute meditation exercise in chapter one designed to teach you how to be still. Earlier in this chapter, we discussed a breathing exercise to help bring relaxation. Both of these can bring relief to the problem of overload in our lives. I'll mention one additional meditation-type activity that the renewal movement calls "soaking." Simply stated:

- Turn on quiet, worshipful music.
- Lie down on the floor or couch using pillows as necessary for comfort.
- Release your thoughts and concerns to God.
- Enjoy being in God's presence.
- Listen in silence for what God may be saying.
- Take time to let God work on you.

A Word About Medications

As with most aspects of health, there is a great temptation for short cuts. The prescription drugs for stress and anxiety are among the most widely prescribed medications in the world. There are a couple of problems with their use, however. First, they are a cover-up. They do not address the cause of the anxiety, and when the cause is not dealt with, healing will not occur. Second, they are highly addictive. Once you start taking Valium, Xanax or Ativan, it is very difficult to stop.

There is a place for them. I had a patient come in one day extremely nervous with a very rapid pulse. He worked with juvenile delinquents and that morning one of the boys in his unit had committed suicide. He was put on one of the anxiolytics for about three or four weeks as he was dealing with this extremely stressful situation. He received counsel as well. Then he was taken off the medication.

Today, we have some alternatives. The new antidepressants like Zoloft, Paxil and Effexor now have indications for anxiety. Another medication called Buspar can also help, and none of these are addictive. It does not take away the need to pursue the root cause but can bring some relief as other steps are taken.

Sometimes anxiety can be a reflection of poor diet choices. Once diet is improved, anxiety may improve significantly. Try to eliminate refined sugar and soft drinks. Replace coffee and other caffeinated beverages with non-caffeinated herbal teas. Consider adding supplements such as calcium, magnesium and B-complex as well as the herbal products kava kava or valerian root. Try these at bedtime initially because they may cause some drowsiness.*

---

* Pregnant and nursing mothers should avoid these. Anyone on chronic medication or with a chronic illness should first check with their medical provider before taking.

Spiritual Connection – Releasing Control to the Prince of Peace

Jesus shows us the Father. The best way for us to know God and His attributes is to know Jesus. He (Jesus) is the image of the invisible God (Col. 1:15). Jesus shows us how to find peace in the storm. He does not promise life will be stress-free, but He gives us His Spirit to dwell in us. He is worthy of our trust. We don't have to stay in a place of fear. We don't have to please everyone. We don't have to fill our life with empty things. We don't have to stuff our feelings. Instead, we can release control to Him. For He Himself is our peace (Eph. 2:14).

Practical Applications – a Brief Review

1. **Begin to unstuff emotions** through exercise, confession, journaling, counseling, breathing and enjoyable outlets.
2. **Confront your fears** and put your trust in God.
3. **Know yourself** – spiritual identity, personality, unique stress symptoms and purpose.
4. **Set healthy boundaries** – learn to say no.
5. **Improve time management.**
6. **Simplify.**
7. **Practice solitude and meditation.**

Recommended Reading

Minirth, M.D., Frank, et al. *How to Beat Burnout.* Chicago: Moody Press, 1986.

Foster, Richard J. *Freedom of Simplicity.* San Francisco:

Harper & Row, 1981.

Anderson, Neil T. *Victory Over the Darkness.* Ventura: Regal Books, 1990.

Rohr, Richard. *Discovering the Enneagram.* New York: Crossroad, 1990.

Covey, Stephen. *The 7 Habits of Highly Effective People.* New York: Simon & Schuster, 1989.

Swenson, M.D., Richard. *Margin: Restoring Emotional, Physical, Financial, and Time Reserves to Overloaded Lives.* Colorado Springs: Navpress, 1992.

CHAPTER THREE

A Biblical Guide to Healthy Eating

Pick up a packaged food in any supermarket and check the ingredients. That tasty-looking item on the box cover or can label may contain anything from chemical preservatives and dyes to unhealthy amounts of saturated fats, refined sugars and salt.

Most of us know such things aren't healthy for us, but we're often like Eve in the Garden of Eden when it comes to food. If it looks pleasing and tastes good, we willingly turn from the path of nutrition, health and longevity to one of instant gratification. The mounting toll of obesity and diet-related cases of heart disease, hypertension and diabetes give grim testimony to our weakness related to food.

"OK," you say. "I know I need to change my diet and lose a few pounds, but does God really care what I eat?" If we study the Bible the only reasonable answer is YES! Food is one of the most basic human needs, and God has supplied our need by providing a huge variety of fruits, vegetables, meats, seeds, roots, nuts, grains and other edibles. Furthermore, the Bible is full of instruction and examples of healthy eating practices, several of which we will examine in this chapter.

The problem with food

Soon after God saved the people of Israel from slavery in Egypt, they started to complain about the provisions on their journey. *If only we had died by the Lord's hand in Egypt!* they cried to Moses. *There we sat around pots of meat and ate all the food we wanted, but you have brought us out into this desert to starve this entire assembly to death* (Exod. 16:3). One of the Israelites' first tests of faith related to food. They had to decide: Are we going to be obedient to the Lord? Are we going to trust that He will provide? Or are we going to do things our way, demanding that God give us what we want and fantasizing about the diet we had in Egypt?

Their description of the Egyptian diet shows some remarkable similarities to the standard American diet. Our *pots of meat* include Big Macs, Whoppers, double-decker tacos, deep fried chicken, enormous pizzas, hot dogs, sausage, bologna and other processed meats. To this, the typical American adds large quantities of high-fat ice cream, cheese, milk, french fries, chocolate, snack foods and butter. And then he washes it all down with coffee, soda or beer.

> "Men dig their graves with their own teeth and die more by those fated instruments than by the weapons of their enemies."
> —*Thomas Moffett, 1600*

The Egyptian diet was actually a cut above its American counterpart, but I use the term to describe our diet because of the similarities. The most striking relates to quantity. The Israelites' description indicates that the Egyptians ate all they wanted. Does that sound familiar? In this land of plenty, we also eat more than our bodies need, and obesity is rampant. Lack of restraint also affects the quality of food we eat. In 1996 alone, Americans spent over $360 billion on junk foods. Since Israel had this same weakness, God began to speak to them about their diet and lifestyle soon after they left Egypt.

He said, "If you listen carefully to the voice of the Lord your God and do what is right in his eyes, if you pay attention to his commands and keep all his decrees, I will not bring on you any of the diseases I brought on the Egyptians, for I am the Lord, who heals you" (Exod. 15:26).

Since the Egyptians suffered from food-related diseases similar to those we have today, it's highly probable we can avoid these diseases by following God's commands related to diet.

The Kosher diet

God's first dietary laws dealt with what kinds of meat to eat and how to prepare them. These laws are detailed in Leviticus chapters 7, 11 and 17 and Deuteronomy 14. Here is a summary of scriptural principles from the Levitical diet, or Kosher diet as we call it now:

1. Do not eat animal fat. *The Lord said to Moses, "Say to the Israelites: 'Do not eat any of the fat of cattle, sheep or goats'"* (Lev. 7:22-23).

2. Do not eat the blood of animals. *And wherever you live, you must not eat the blood of any bird or animal* (Lev. 7:26).

3. Do not eat animals or creatures classified as unclean. *You must therefore make a distinction between clean and unclean animals and between unclean and clean birds. Do not defile yourselves by any animal or bird or anything that moves along the ground – those which I have set apart as unclean for you* (Lev. 20:25).

4. When an animal is found dead, it is unclean, and its carcass can cause cooking utensils or other things it comes in contact with to be unclean (Lev. 11:32-35).

Notice there is no mention of the four basic food groups or number of servings. We know that the Jewish diet was a starch-centered diet with bread as its main staple. Yet the regulations in this diet have to do with animals – the fat, the blood, the clean, the unclean. Why is there no mention of fruits or vegetables, grains and starches? One possible reason is that there was no need for regulations or restrictions of these foods. They could be enjoyed without limit.

Why were there regulations regarding the meat in their diet? One probable reason is that through animal products, harmful bacteria could be introduced into the body. The strict Levitical regulations helped them avoid this menace. Let's look at the distinctions between clean and unclean animals, for example (see Lev. 11).

Is there any rhyme or reason to the way God separates the clean and unclean animals? Yes, creatures are generally classified by whether or not they are scavengers. An animal, bird or fish that is a scavenger will eat most anything, including dead animals, rotting foods or even their own waste. They are the garbage disposals of the animal kingdom, and this is not a bad thing. We need scavengers in this world to help remove the waste products. We need vultures to eat the carcasses of other animals. We need shellfish to help clean up the waste produced by other marine life. We need the pigs and rabbits and badgers to do their thing. But we would be well advised **not** to eat the meat of these creatures ourselves. As scavengers, they are far more likely to harbor substances that are disease-producing in man – substances like the trichinosis nematode found in pork or the toxins in shellfish.

KOSHER MEAT CHART		
	CLEAN	**UNCLEAN**
Animals	Cow Sheep Deer Goat	Rabbit Camel Swine (includes pork, bacon, and ham)
General rule for mammals: *If has a split hoof <u>and</u> chews the cud, it is clean.*		
Fish	Bass Mackerel Cod Perch Flounder Sole Grouper Salmon Haddock Red Snapper Halibut Trout Herring Tuna	Shark Swordfish Catfish Shrimp Lobster Crabs Clams Scallops Snails Oysters Mussels
General rule for fish: *If has fins and scales, it is clean.*		

KOSHER MEAT CHART

	CLEAN	UNCLEAN
Birds	Chicken Turkey Duck Quail Cornish Hen	Eagle Owl Vulture Sea Gull Buzzard Hawk Falcon Stork Raven Bat Ostrich
Insects	Locust Cricket Grasshopper	All Others

General rule for **all creatures:** *If it is not a scavenger, it is clean. If it is a scavenger, it is unclean.*

Most likely, God instructed the people to drain the blood from clean animals for the same reason. Blood is a common source of disease-causing germs. In Deuteronomy 12:23-25, God says:

> *But be sure you do not eat the blood, because the blood is the life, and you must not eat the life with the meat. You must not eat the blood; pour it out on the ground like water. Do not eat it, so that it may go well with you and your children after you, because you will be doing what is right in the eyes of the Lord.*

As for the regulations regarding animal carcasses, the obvious reason behind this is to avoid infectious disease. When an animal dies, its body soon decomposes through scavenger-type microorganisms. We all know the dangers of eating meat that has been unrefrigerated and not fresh. But bacteria and microorganisms were not discovered until relatively recently. The biblical regulations regarding this and other sanitary laws were centuries ahead of their time. (See Numbers 19 regarding hand washing and Deuteronomy 23:12-13 regarding proper disposal of human waste.)

The regulation to not eat animal fat is another obviously inspired guideline. *This is a lasting ordinance for the generations to come, wherever you live: You must not eat any fat...* (Lev. 3:17). Medical research since the 1950's has shown the dangers of ingesting animal fat. When we eat animal fat, our blood cells can more easily stick together and form clots which can lead to heart attacks, strokes, pulmonary embolism and deep venous thrombosis. Fats promote the growth of cancer cells and can contribute to the development of adult-onset diabetes and obesity.[18] This is one area where modern research is finally catching up to the truths found in Scripture.

One danger in eating meats today that our Bible forefathers did not face is chemical toxins. Researchers from the National Academy of Sciences report that beef contains the highest concentration of herbicides of any food sold in America. The source of these herbicides is the corn and soybeans the cattle are fed. Similarly, beef ranks high on the list of foods posing the greatest health risk due to pesticide contamination.[19,20] Since these contaminants are fat-soluble, they concentrate in the flesh of the animal (chicken, cow, fish, etc.). When we consume the flesh, we take in these contaminants. Nearly all cattle receive growth hormones and steroids to quicken growth. Many also receive antibiotics to fight disease. All of these drugs can be passed on to humans through the meat. Other meats and fish are similarly susceptible. So the next time you want a steak, consider what might be in it.

The Daniel Diet

Daniel and his three friends came from the royal family of Israel, where they no doubt dined on the best foods of their culture. But after being carried off as slaves to Babylon, they no longer could freely choose their diet. They were trained for service in the royal court, and as part of their preparation, they were required to eat food from the king's table (Dan. 1).

Daniel knew this food included meats forbidden by the Levitical law, so rather than defile his body, he proposed a test. He and his three friends would eat only vegetables and drink only water for 10 days. After the 10 days, they compared their appearance with those who ate the king's rich food, and they won easily. They look healthier and better nourished than the others, so soon everyone's diet was switched to vegetarian.

What was wrong with the royal diet? Obviously there was something in it which would have caused Daniel to be defiled, most likely blood, fat or unclean meat. Because they could not get a Kosher diet, Daniel and his friends chose to eat no meat at all. Their story illustrates how we can respond to cultural pressures related to food. In our own culture, advertisements on TV, radio or on billboards constantly entice us to eat rich foods. Daniel and his friends must have been under intense pressure to conform to the Babylonian ways, but because they believed the Lord would reward their obedience, they willingly put their lives on the line.

In the early 1900s, Yale University professor Irving Fisher conducted an experiment that compared the strength and stamina of meat-eaters with vegetarians through a series of tests. He found that what was true for Daniel and his friends back in ancient Babylon is true today as well. *Of the three groups compared, the... flesh-eaters showed far less endurance than the abstainers [vegetarians], even when the latter were leading a sedentary life.*[21] A study done in 1968 by a team of Danish researchers produced similar results. The subjects of the study were placed on a mixed diet of meat and vegetables for a period of time, and then tested on a stationary bicycle. Later, they were fed a diet high in meat, milk and eggs for a similar period and then re-tested. Finally, they were fed a strict vegetarian diet, and tested again. Their endurance was best (more than double) on the vegetarian diet![22]

One common myth is that rich people, because of their access to the best foods, are better nourished than poor people. I believe it is by God's great design that some of the most nutritious foods are commonly available to both rich and poor. People who routinely eat rich food (the typical American diet) are much more likely to be plagued with diseases such as hypertension, coronary artery disease, osteoarthritis, diabetes, strokes, cancer and obesity. People who eat simple food (beans, potatoes, corn, whole-grain breads, vegetables and fruit) are more likely to be free from these diseases. Proverbs 23:1-3 says, *When you sit to dine with a ruler, note well what is before you, and put a knife to your throat if you are given to gluttony. Do not crave his delicacies, for that food is deceptive.*

In the past, "rich foods" were only available to the wealthy. A century ago, the arthritic condition commonly known as gout was seen only in people of wealth because only they could afford the rich foods that caused it. Today, it is spreading because these foods are now normal daily fare for western civilization. Dr. John McDougall, who has written several books on the connection between food and disease, defines rich foods to include

> ...*red meat, poultry, eggs, fish, shellfish, cheeses, milk, oils, nuts, seeds, white rice, refined flour, processed foods, salt and sugar. They were traditionally found in abundance only on festive occasions. The unfortunate reality is that, in one form or another, most westerners feast at each and every meal, twenty-one times or more a week.*[23]

Our culture often elevates these delicacies by describing them as food "to die for." Unfortunately, that is an accurate description.

The Eden Diet

Then God said, "I give you every seed-bearing plant on the face of the whole earth and every tree that has fruit with seed in it. They will be yours for food" (Gen. 1:29). It can be fun to imagine what life was like for Adam and Eve in the garden. Their idyllic life was without the cares and stresses of our fast-paced culture. No headaches regarding neighbors – they had no neighbors. No stress at the office – they were outdoors tending the garden. No time commitments – what's the rush when you live over 900 years? No sickness or disease – for there was no sin – yet. No competition for designer clothes – for there were no clothes! And where is the stress in food preparation when you can walk up to (almost) any tree and have an instant meal without worrying about pesticides, herbicides or clean-up? Who needs a dishwasher?

When we talk about going back to basics, here is about as far back as we can go. What was the original diet? The answer lies in Genesis 1:29: seed-bearing plants and fruits. This would include all vegetables, grains, nuts and fruits. They are God's gift to us.

The original diet was a vegetarian diet for Adam and Eve, for Cain, Abel, Seth and so on – all the way to Noah. After the flood, God allowed Noah and his family to eat meat, though He prohibited the eating of blood.

Was the original diet healthy? Obviously, yes. It would be the "manufacturer's" specific recommendation. At that time an average life span was 900 years! (See chart).

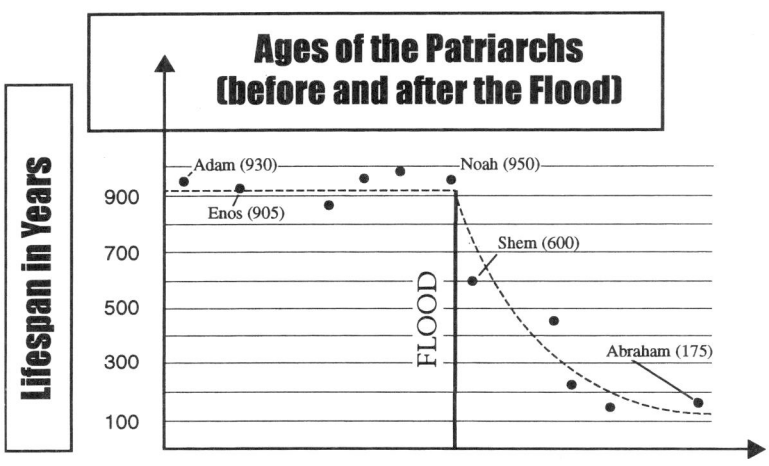

Obviously, there are many factors besides diet to be considered when studying their longevity, but all of these near "millennialites" were vegetarians. Looking at the chart again, you can see that after the flood the average life span suddenly tapered down to around 120 years. This was predictable from what God says 100 years before the flood: *My Spirit will not contend with man forever, for he is mortal; his days will be a hundred and twenty years* (Gen. 6:3).

> "The cultures with the very longest life spans in the world are the Vilicambas, who reside in the Andes of Ecuador, the Abkhasians, who live on the Black Sea, and the Hunzas, who live in the Himalayas of northern Pakistan... All three are either totally vegetarian or close to it."
>
> —*John Robbins*
> *in* Diet for a New America

How did God so dramatically change man's life span? One major factor was the atmospheric change that took place after the flood. Without as much water vapor in the sky, harmful ultraviolet radiation began to penetrate through the earth's ozone shield. I believe another factor was allowing man to now eat flesh.

Common Myths About Food

The issues of diet and nutrition seem to invite controversy, quackery and faddishness. The terrible paradox in our culture between our obsession with eating and our desire to be thin and healthy makes us willing to try almost any new diet plan. And because so many have tried – and failed – there are about as many opinions as there are diet plans.

Some people tout low-carbohydrate, high-protein plans like the Atkins or Stillman diets. Others who want rapid weight loss go for liquid protein diets or the near-starvation diets that athletes sometimes use. Then there are the high-fiber, low-protein diets like the Pritiken diet. Today the most popular are low-fat, low-cholesterol diets. But which of these is going to work best? And which is the safest and healthiest? There are no quick answers. It's especially confusing because each new diet seems to have a medical doctor endorsing it. We tend to think that doctors have all the answers about health issues, but when it comes to nutrition, physicians are not necessarily the best-informed. A Senate subcommittee once looked into how much nutrition instruction the average U.S.-trained physician receives in medical school. The shocking answer is less than three hours.[24]

The confusion has been made worse because of myths about nutrition that have been spread by the country's powerful meat and dairy industries. Numerous medical studies have shown that what these industries are telling us about the healthfulness of their products simply isn't true. Despite this evidence, scientists, doctors and dietitians have failed to actively challenge the prevailing myths. They excuse their silence by saying that literature on nutrition is still too sketchy or controversial. However, when the scientific studies are examined with an open mind, the strong link between rich foods and our chronic health problems is undeniable. As for controversy, yes, it is unpopular to preach against meat and dairy products. People love these products; our economy thrives on them; and it's our choice to consume them. These same arguments were used by supporters of the tobacco industry with tragic results.

By examining common myths about food and checking the facts, we'll confirm that the Bible's approach to eating is really the most healthful and sensible after all.

Myth #1 – We need to eat meat to get enough protein.

Everyone knows how important protein is in our diet. We need protein to provide the building materials for muscles, hormones and enzymes. The meat industry would have us believe that a diet lacking meat cannot possibly provide enough protein to maintain our health. The truth is that even vegetarians get more than enough protein in their diets. Nutritional studies as early as 1950 have shown that adults need between 2.5 to 5 percent of their daily caloric intake to be in protein form. Taking the 5 percent figure, this would be about 30 to 40 grams of protein for the average man or woman.

It would be nearly impossible **not** to get this quantity of protein if you're meeting these daily caloric standards, even as a vegetarian. For example, the percentage of calories provided by protein in spinach is 49 percent; broccoli, 45 percent; cauliflower, 40 percent; lettuce, 35 percent; peas, 30 percent; green beans, 26 percent; cucumbers, 24 percent; celery, 21 percent; potatoes, 11 percent; sweet potatoes, 6 percent; cantaloupe, 9 percent; strawberries, 8 percent; orange, 8 percent; watermelon, 8 percent; peach, 6 percent; pear, 5 percent; banana, 5 percent; and apple 1 percent.[25]

Though we need just 30-40 grams of protein a day, the average American consumes over 100 grams! Now we might argue that if 30-40 grams is adequate, then why wouldn't 100 grams be better? Because excess protein leads to the leaching of calcium from our bones and is a major cause of osteoporosis. The higher the protein intake, the more common is osteoporosis. For example, Eskimos have an extremely high protein intake (250-400 grams a day) and have one of the highest rates of osteoporosis in the world.[26] On the other hand, the African Bantus consume 47 grams of protein and only 400 mg of calcium a day, yet are essentially free of osteoporosis.[27]

> "One farmer says to me,
> 'You cannot live on vegetable food solely,
> for it furnishes nothing to make bones
> with.' And all the while,
> he walks behind oxen, which,
> with vegetable-made bones,
> jerk him and his lumbering plow along
> in spite of every obstacle."
> —*Henry David Thoreau*

Excess protein can also contribute to calcium kidney stones. The leached calcium from the bones is filtered out of the blood by the kidneys, which increases the concentration of calcium in the urine. Excess protein can also lead to the destruction of kidney tissue and eventually to a loss of kidney function. One of the first things recommended by most nephrologists (kidney specialists) for patients with moderate to severe kidney disease is to change to a low protein diet.

Other studies have implicated excess protein with cancer and diabetes. T. Colin Campbell, a Professor of Nutritional Sciences at Cornell University and the senior science advisor to the American Institute for Cancer Research, says there is *a strong correlation between dietary protein intake and cancer of the breast, prostate, pancreas, and colon.*[28]

Consider this. The U.S. Government recommendation on daily protein consumption was 118 grams earlier in this century. In the 1980s it dropped to 46-56 grams. In 1990, it dropped to 25-35 grams. Today, look at any nutrition label and you will discover that a recommended daily amount of protein is not even listed! This is because nutritionists now know it would be extremely unlikely that a person would not meet their protein requirements.

Myth #2 – Animal foods contain protein that is superior to plant proteins.

This fallacy was based on experiments conducted on rats in 1914 and in the 1940s. In 1914, Osborn and Mendel discovered that rats grew better on animal sources of protein than on vegetable sources.[29] In the 1940s, researchers discovered that ten amino acids were essential for a rat's diet. Animal products contained these amino acids in just the right proportions.[30]

The problem is that humans are not rats, and what a rat thrives on is different than what a human thrives on. For instance, when you compare human breast milk with rat's milk there is a large difference in the proportion of protein calories (49 percent for rats and only 5 percent for humans). Obviously, we have different nutritional needs. In 1952, experiments were done by William Rose which determined that humans required only eight essential amino acids and that vegetables and fruits are an excellent source of all of them.[31]

Food combining is also a related myth which states that it is necessary to combine certain vegetables (like corn and beans), to give you complete protein. This is totally unnecessary and only complicates meal planning. Dr. Alfred Harper, chairman of Nutritional Sciences at the University of Wisconsin, Madison, wrote, *One of the biggest fallacies ever perpetuated is that there is any need for so-called complete protein.*[32]

Myth #3 – You need to eat dairy products to get enough calcium.

Everyone knows that milk and dairy products build strong bones and teeth. At least, that is what we have been told. Yet most people in the world have diets that do not include any dairy products at all. Cow's milk – portrayed as nature's perfect food for humans – is actually the perfect food for calves. McDougall writes, *No other animal* [talking about man] *in its natural environment drinks milk after it is weaned. Furthermore, in nature no young animal drinks the milk of another species.*[33] When cow's milk is fed exclusively to cows (past the age of weaning), sickness and death occurs within months.

Here are five solid scientific reasons to avoid milk and dairy products:

1. They are the leading cause of food allergies.
2. A large percentage of people past the age of four lose the ability to digest the lactose found in milk.
3. Unsafe levels of environmental contaminants (such as pesticides and antibiotics) tend to accumulate in dairy products.
4. High calcium diets have been associated with calcium kidney stones.
5. Dairy products are high in fat and contain no fiber.

God designed the body to be a very efficient regulator of calcium. If the diet is low in calcium, absorption is increased. If the diet is high, absorption is decreased.

In fact, writes McDougall, *calcium deficiency caused by an insufficient amount of calcium in the diet is not known to occur in humans, even though most people in the world don't drink milk after weaning because of custom, lactose intolerance, or unavailability.*[34]

Myth #4 – Humans are carnivorous.

Is man designed to be an herbivore (plant eater) or a carnivore (meat eater)? When we compare the anatomy and physiology of our bodies with animals who are exclusively herbivores or exclusively carnivores, there are some interesting revelations. Carnivores have teeth designed to tear apart raw meat. The majority of our teeth are flat for grinding grains and vegetables. Our saliva contains an enzyme called alpha-amylase which breaks down the complex carbohydrates found in plant foods. Carnivorous animals lack this enzyme in their saliva. Our saliva is also highly alkaline which helps buffer the stomach and duodenum from becoming too acidic and protecting against ulcers. Carnivores' saliva and digestive secretions are highly acidic to the point of being able to dissolve the bones of their prey.

> "Although we think we are one,
> and we act as if we are one,
> human beings are not natural carnivores...
> When we kill animals to eat them,
> they end up killing us because
> their flesh was never intended for human
> beings, who are naturally herbivores."
> —*William C. Roberts, M.D.*
> *Editor in chief,*
> *American Journal of Cardiology*

The rest of the digestive tract also shows distinctions. Herbivores have long intestines which are rippled, allowing them more time and a larger surface area to digest the nutrients found in plants. Carnivores have short, smooth intestinal tracts which allow them to rapidly digest and eliminate the decomposing flesh. Our intestinal tract is long and rippled. Clearly God designed our bodies for a more vegetarian than meat-centered diet.

A worldwide diet pattern

In studying the diets of cultures around the world, one common thread throughout history is that diets have been starch-centered. Their primary foods are not meat, but complex carbohydrates. For Asians it's rice. For natives of North and Central America it's corn. For those in Western Europe it's bread and potatoes. In South America and Africa it's grains and beans. In the South Pacific it's sweet potatoes. God placed in each of these areas a nutritious, starch-based food that would satisfy dietary needs. Though this has changed as areas have become more industrialized, it's still commonplace throughout the world.

Countries that Americans think of as poor and underdeveloped commonly have a more healthful overall diet than we. In these starch-eating cultures we find little evidence of the most common American diseases (hypertension, diabetes, heart disease, stroke, arthritis and cancer). When we do find disease and illness in these countries, it is more often related to a lack of food or poor sanitation.

A Diet for All Diseases

Selecting the right diet for my patients used to be quite complicated. I had specific diets to treat various ailments. There was the low-salt diet for hypertension, the low-fat diet for hyperlipidemia, the low-purine diet for gout, the low-sugar diet for diabetes, and the low-protein diet for kidney disease. Besides all of these, there were the scores of weight loss diets promoted by every movie star, physician or athlete imaginable.

Now I use one simple diet that works for all the diseases listed above (and others too). The diet is starch-centered, with lots of vegetables and fruits, and avoidance of rich foods. This diet fits the biblical pattern of the Eden and Daniel diets, and now there is ample medical evidence to support it. For example:

Hypertension – A diet low in sodium, fat and animal products and high in fiber (the starch-centered diet), has been shown to lower elevated blood pressure. In fact, hypertension is virtually unknown in countries where the intake of sodium, fat and cholesterol is low. John McDougall M.D. noticed that when mild to moderate hypertensive patients came to his live-in health program and were started on this particular diet, most could be taken off their medications in 1-2 days![35]

Heart disease and hyperlipidemia – Numerous studies have conclusively linked a high fat diet with heart disease, stroke and peripheral vascular disease. These same diseases improve or are prevented when a starch-centered diet is followed. One impressive study involving 24,000 people found the heart disease mortality rate for lacto-ovo vegetarians (those who eat dairy and egg) to be only one-third that

> "A vegetarian diet can prevent 90 to 97% of heart disease."
> —*Journal of the American Medical Association*

of meat eaters, and pure vegetarians only one-tenth that of meat eaters![36]

Diabetes – When adult-onset diabetic patients are restricted to a low-fat, high-fiber (starch-centered), diet, up to 70 percent of those on insulin no longer need it and an even larger percentage of those on pills can be freed from their medication.[37] John Robbins, author of *Diet for A New America*, writes, *Worldwide, the disease is rare or nonexistent among peoples whose diets are primarily grains, vegetables and fruits. If these same people switch to rich meat-based diets, however, their incidence of diabetes balloons.*[38]

Arthritis – The official position of the Arthritis Foundation is that diet and arthritis are not related. However, the limited studies done on this subject indicate an improvement in arthritic patients who were put on a low-fat diet. When we look at the people in parts of the world where this starch-centered diet is followed, arthritis is rare even among the elderly.

Cancer – The respected medical journal, *Advances in Cancer Research*, states: *At present, we have overwhelming evidence...* (that) *none of the risk factors for cancer is... more significant than diet and nutrition.*[39] And yes, a diet low in fat and high in fiber has been shown to protect or significantly lower one's chances of acquiring this dreaded disease.

Obesity – The same diet applies to this ubiquitous problem. Dr. Jean Mayer, a renowned Harvard nutritionist said, *In becoming a vegetarian, you will eat a greater percentage of your calories from cereal grains, dried beans and peas, potatoes and pasta – the very foods most dieters avoid with zeal. And you will lose weight.*[40]

Other diseases – The list could go on to include kidney stones, kidney failure, gallstones, anemia, asthma, ulcer, constipation and irritable bowel syndrome. The same diet, the same healthy results.

> "Food is your best medicine, and the best food is the best medicine."
> —*Hippocrates*

So, why did God allow meat?

With all the evidence on the health benefits of a vegetarian, starch-centered "Eden Diet," the inevitable question must be, why did God allow the addition of meat to the human diet after the flood? We can only speculate here. Prior to the flood, God was deeply grieved and angry over the human race's sinfulness. So in Genesis 6:3 God declared a 120-year limit on the human life span (in the pre-flood world, men were living up to nine centuries). By adding meat to their diet, he not only decreased man's life expectancy because of the factors already mentioned, but adds a dimension of fear and danger into the food-gathering process. Animals are now afraid of man, and there is some danger in stalking them.

Another example in Scripture more clearly shows God allowing meat in response to man's sinfulness. After the Israelites left Egypt and were safely across the Red Sea, God began to miraculously provide manna (a starch-centered food) for them to eat. But soon they began complaining, remembering the meat they had in Egypt. *But now we have lost our appetite; we never see anything but this manna!* (Num. 11:6). The Lord's response is worth quoting:

> *The Lord heard you when you wailed, "If only we had meat to eat! We were better off in Egypt!" Now the Lord will give you meat, and you will eat it. You will not eat it for just one day, or two days, or five, ten or twenty days, but for a whole month – until it comes out*

of your nostrils and you loathe it – because you have rejected the Lord, who is among you, and have wailed before him, saying, "Why did we ever leave Egypt?" (Num. 11:18-20)

Because of man's persistence, the Lord allows him to have his way – and to suffer the consequences. For example, when the Israelites gorged themselves on the quail the Lord miraculously provided, a plague struck them. Today, as the American people overload on meat, eggs and dairy products, a plague is striking them. It is not instantaneous. It is not obvious to the casual observer, but it is taking its toll in heart disease, hypertension and other maladies. Industries which profit from meat and dairy products don't want us to know the truth about the long-term use of these foods. They promote them as healthful, protein-rich foods and attempt to counter any link between their products and disease. All the while, people are dying prematurely, and we are led to believe it is part of the normal aging process.

> "Think of the fierce energy concentrated in an acorn! You bury it in the ground, and it explodes into a giant oak! You bury a sheep, and nothing happens but decay!"
> —*George Bernard Shaw*

Legalism and Other Tough Questions

Most Scripture references used in this chapter have come from the Old Testament and more specifically, the law of Moses. God gave these regulations to the people of Israel to protect them from the consequences of sin. If they obeyed

His law, there was blessing. If they disobeyed, there was a curse. Today, we are not under law, but under grace. Galatians 3:23-25 says,

> *Before this faith came, we were held prisoners by the law, locked up until faith should be revealed. So the law was put in charge to lead us to Christ that we might be justified by faith. Now that faith has come, we are no longer under the supervision of the law.*

So how do we handle the question of whether to obey Old Testament dietary laws? It's helpful to look at some key verses about food from the New Testament.

> *...do not worry about your life, what you will eat; or about your body, what you will wear. Life is more than food, and the body more than clothes... And do not set your heart on what you will eat or drink; do not worry about it. For the pagan world runs after all such things, and your Father knows that you need them. But seek his kingdom, and these things will be given to you as well* (Luke 12:22-31).

There is a difference between worrying about food and making wise choices. Certainly seeking God and His kingdom is supreme, though when we seek His kingdom, we might seek His will regarding how we are to eat.

> *"Don't you see that nothing that enters a man from the outside can make him 'unclean'? For it doesn't go into his heart but into his stomach, and then out of his body." In saying this, Jesus declared all foods "clean"* (Mark 7:18-19).

In His response to the Pharisees here, Jesus made it clear that we are not saved or condemned by the food we eat. Sin is what makes us spiritually unclean.

> *He who regards one day as special, does so to the Lord. He who eats meat, eats to the Lord, for he gives thanks to God; and he who abstains, does so to the Lord and gives thanks to God (Rom. 14:6). Therefore let us stop passing judgment on one another. Instead, make up your mind not to put any stumbling block or obstacle in your brother's way. As one who is in the Lord Jesus, I am fully convinced that no food is unclean in itself (Rom. 14:13,14).*

The main point of this portion of Scripture is verse 17: *For the kingdom of God is not a matter of eating and drinking, but of righteousness, peace and joy in the Holy Spirit.*

> *But food does not bring us near to God; we are no worse if we do not eat, and no better if we do (1 Cor. 8:8).*

This Scripture, like the previous one, is dealing with food sacrificed to idols. The main point, I believe, is again that food is not a spiritual litmus test.

> *The Spirit clearly says in later times some will abandon the faith and follow deceiving spirits and things taught by demons.... They forbid people to marry and order them to abstain from certain foods, which God created to be received with thanksgiving by those who believe and who know the truth (1 Tim. 4:1-3).*

These verses show Paul's concerns about the harshness of legalism. With all the scientific support and some supporting Scriptures, it would be easy to return to Mt. Sinai and develop a law that kills instead of restoring life as it was intended.

Frankly, I cannot look at the Scriptures and say: "God wants us to avoid meat and eat a vegetarian diet." I think there are Scriptures that support this. I think the scientific evidence is overwhelming. I think if people did, it would make a tremendous difference in their physical health and well-being. But it must be an individual decision borne out of our convictions about what the Lord is saying to us personally.

Three Points of Biblical Guidance on Food

These are the key points that I believe the Bible is teaching us about food:

1. The original diet God gave to humankind was vegetarian with lots of raw fruits and vegetables. Man's longevity and lack of illness during those early years were partly a reflection of being on this diet.

2. God allowed man to eat meat after the flood, and further clarified in the Mosaic Law that it was to come from "clean" animals. Meat was primarily a feast food.

3. Food is not a factor in our salvation, spiritual maturity or acceptance by God. Our personal food choices should not be made into legalistic regulations.

Recommendations

Most medical professionals today recommend some form of low-fat, low-cholesterol diet. Ironically, this diet has similarities to the Levitical (Kosher) diet that God ordained centuries ago. A growing portion of health organizations are also beginning to recommend a more vegetarian diet – much like the Daniel or Eden diet we described earlier.

> "*Food Groups You Cannot Eat:*
> Meat, milk, cheese, butter, desserts,
> processed foods, fried foods,
> foods with skins, restaurant food,
> foods your mom made,
> foods from packages,
> foods shown in commercials,
> foods containing flavor, breakfast,
> lunch, dinner, take-out, drive-thru.
> *Food Groups You Can Eat:*
> Water (unsweetened), low-fat celery,
> woodchips."
>
> —Dave Berry
> *syndicated humor columnist*

Here are my own recommendations:

1. **Evaluate your diet.** If you picture your body as God's temple, then ask yourself if the building materials you are using to maintain it are of poor, adequate or high quality. Ask God for wisdom here. If you have a family history of heart disease or cancer, start changing your diet to help prevent these diseases in your own body. Even if your family medical history lacks these risk factors, there are still ample reasons to choose the best building blocks for your temple.

2. **Start making changes, even small ones.** Most of us know we need to improve on how we feed our bodies. We want to make the changes described here, but feel overwhelmed about how to begin. Don't panic. Small changes can make a difference. If you suffer

from a chronic illness such as high blood pressure, diabetes, heart disease or arthritis and are highly motivated, consider a more sudden and radical change to a starch-centered vegetarian diet. If not, consider a more gradual change. Consider moving toward the Kosher diet first. Cut back or avoid unclean animals. Reduce consumption of meat and dairy foods. Then move toward the Daniel diet. Begin to eat more fruits and vegetables. Use water as your primary liquid. Use fewer processed foods. Begin to replace meat with starches (baked potatoes, whole grain breads and pastas, beans, brown rice and corn). If you feel ready, then move toward the Eden diet – eliminating meat and dairy completely, and eating more of your fruits and vegetables fresh and raw.

3. **Have starches readily available.** This is crucial to the success of this lifestyle change. If you don't eat enough starches, you won't get enough calories. You'll constantly be hungry and most likely want to go back to your old way of eating. To encourage you to replace meat with starches, it helps to have a few choices available. For instance, bake 5-10 potatoes per person to last up to one week. I have acquired a taste for cold baked potatoes, but you might prefer to warm them. Similarly, cook a pot of brown rice and during the week you can easily add raw or steamed vegetables to it. A pot of beans or whole grain pasta can work the same way. Having whole grain breads and rolls on hand is another great starch choice. If it is within your budget, consider buying a bread machine. When corn is in season, this is also another

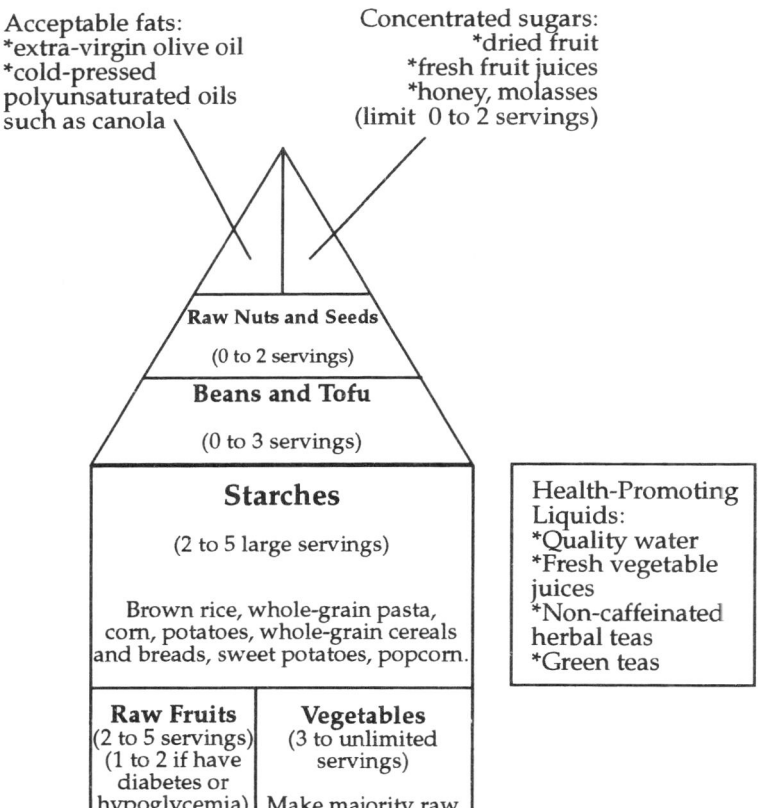

The Temple Foods Chart

superb starch. Remember that what you add to the starch is important. There are healthy alternatives to butter, sour cream and cheese for your baked potato. Try beans, salsa or marinara sauce instead.

4. **Eat more fresh vegetables and fruit.** Fruits and vegetables are high in antioxidant vitamins and minerals which can help neutralize or remove the disease causing "free radicals" that can invade our bodies. Organically grown produce is best and lessens your exposure to chemicals. If eaten raw you also ingest the active enzymes that are naturally present which help in the digestion of the fruit or vegetable. God wonderfully supplies these enzymes in all foods, but cooking usually destroys them. The National Cancer Institute and the U.S. Dept. of Health and Human Services recommend at least five servings a day. A great way to start is to eat a large fresh salad once or twice a day, one which includes a wide variety of raw vegetables and a limited amount of dressing. Another way is by using a juice extractor. Consider investing in one and having a fresh glass of vegetable juice once or twice a day.

5. **Decrease fats.** By now you know that animal fats are harmful, but if you simply replace animal fats with other varieties, you won't have gained much ground. Margarine, for example, is vegetable oil that has been chemically altered, creating a group of fats called trans-fats. These have been more strongly linked to cancer and heart disease than some of the animal fats. The best idea is to reduce all fats. Start by drastically reducing or eliminating animal fats (meats, dairy,

eggs). The Bible recommends olive oil, although you should limit your consumption. "Extra-virgin" olive oil is the best. Other oils that may be included are canola, corn and safflower (especially if cold-pressed).

6. **Drink more water.** Stormie Omartian devotes a whole chapter in her book, *Greater Health God's Way,* to this subject. She points out that increasing your water intake is one of the simplest and most effective preventative health steps. Our bodies are nearly 70 percent water and the best liquid for us to ingest is pure, plain water. Find out about your water supply and if necessary consider distilled water or a filtration system for your kitchen. Make it your goal to drink a 16-ounce glass before each meal and before bedtime (64 ounces total). You'll need more in hot weather or when exercising. Other drink alternatives include fresh vegetable juices or herbal and green teas (non-caffeinated). Regular soft drinks have excessive amounts of sugar and diet drinks are full of chemicals. Rice, almond or soy milk (found in health food stores) can be used as a substitute for cow's milk.

7. **Decrease or eliminate foods made with refined flour, sugar and salt.** If the food is in a package, chances are good that it contains one or all of the above. Learn to read labels. These are common ingredients in most processed foods and the nutritional value is almost nil, thus often described as "empty calories." The main problem with refined grains is the removal of most of the vitamins and fiber. Refined sugar products can lead to dental cavities, obesity and a weak-

ened immune system. Excess salt can increase blood pressure and cause fluid retention. Your health can improve simply by avoiding these three white substances – flour, sugar and salt.

8. **Consider nutritional supplements.** These do not replace a good healthy diet, but can complement it. I recommend using them while transitioning to a healthier diet or when your health is already compromised. With the depletion of minerals from our soil, food often has less nutritive value than we think. There are some excellent "whole food" supplements available which I recommend over the less expensive drugstore variety, which are often derived from petroleum products. Everyone can benefit from taking an antioxidant formula. For adults, this could include Vitamin C (500-2000 mg per day), Vitamin E (400-800 IU per day), and selenium (50-100 mcg). There is also great benefit in taking in 400-800 mcg of folic acid, since a deficiency has been directly linked to birth defects and a greater risk of heart attacks. If you follow a strict vegan diet (no meat or dairy products), you will need to eat foods fortified with Vitamin B_{12}, or take a supplement containing it. If you are eating a meal that is completely cooked, a high quality digestive enzyme can bring great support to your body.

9. **Do further reading.** It's worth the effort to find out how food can help rather than hurt your health. Here are five good resources:

- *The McDougall Plan* by John McDougall, MD, New Win Publishing, 1983. This book addresses the dangers of the standard American diet, the benefits of a vegetarian, starch-centered diet and references various scientific studies to back up its claims.

- *The McDougall Program – 12 Days to Dynamic Health* also by McDougall, NAL/Plume Books, 1991. This book gives specific and practical steps on how to change to a healthier diet.

- *Diet For a New America* by John Robbins, Stillpoint Publishing, 1987. This book addresses similar issues to those in McDougall's book, but includes an animal rights perspective. It raises disturbing questions about how the meat industry treats animals it raises for food.

- *The Genesis Diet* by Gordon Tessler, Well Publications, 1996. This book makes a good case for all Christians to follow the Kosher diet, and it describes additional benefits of the Eden diet.

- *God's Way to Ultimate Health* by George Malkmus, Hallelujah Acres Publishing, 1995. This book, written from a Christian perspective, promotes an Eden-type diet with its emphasis on raw fruits and vegetables, distilled water, carrot juice and a powdered supplement called Barley Green. Some people who follow this diet may need to add more starches.

Here are four highly recommended cookbooks:

- *Weimar Institute's Newstart Lifestyle Cookbook* by Sally J. Christenson and Frances De Vries, Thomas Nelson Publishers, 1997.

- *Diet for a New World* by John Robbins, Avon Books, 1992.

- *The American Vegetarian Cookbook: From the Fit for Life Kitchen* by Marilyn Diamond, Warner Books, 1990.
- *Recipes for Life: From God's Garden* by Rhonda Malkmus, Hallelujah Acres Publishing, 1998.

10. **Get support.** Making a major change in your diet is not easy, but is worth it. Having the support of a friend or family member can make a big difference in your success.

The Spiritual Connection – Feasting with the Lord of the Harvest

Just as our physical hunger and thirst should be satisfied with good food and drink, so also should our spirits be fed the best spiritual food. Jesus said, *I am the bread of life. He who comes to me will never go hungry, and he who believes in me will never be thirsty* (John 6:35). Never is an extreme. It reflects an eternal promise. And what a wonderful guarantee!

At the point of Jesus' death on a cross, relationship with God became accessible to all. And Jesus instructs us to remember His death through the eating of the bread (which represents His body), and the drinking of the wine (which represents His blood).

The invitation God gives us is to come, to believe, to commune. "All things are ready, come to the feast!"

CHAPTER FOUR

A Fast Track to Health – Exercise

One of my patients, a middle-aged man named Doug,* is hooked on golf. He loves to play whenever and wherever he can. So when his golf instructor blurted out one day, "You are too fat and tight to get an appropriate golf swing," it got his attention fast.

Inwardly, Doug knew that his increasing girth was driving a wedge between him and his weekend passion. He also knew that because of his age (45), weight (250), and a recently diagnosed thyroid condition, that losing weight wasn't going to be easy. Yet, he was highly motivated. He had already quit smoking, and soon he started a serious exercise program.

He began slowly riding a stationary bicycle. At first he

---

* Not the same person as the mechanic in chapter one.

could only last a few minutes before he was exhausted. By the end of a year, he was able to ride for an entire hour. Then he started using a treadmill, at first walking, then gradually jogging on it, and finally jogging outdoors. At the same time he began using dumbbells and weight machines to increase his strength, and stretching exercises to increase his flexibility. He made significant diet changes as well – eating more of a Daniel-type vegetarian diet and juicing lots of fresh vegetables – but he felt his most important lifestyle change was regular exercise.

The benefits he has experienced are numerous: increased energy and self-confidence, no more constipation, no more joint pain, improved body odor and a size 32 waist. However, his two favorite benefits are increased flexibility to swing a golf club "appropriately" and the stamina to walk 36 holes in one day.

Probably no health habit pays bigger and quicker dividends than exercise. Within a few days of starting an exercise program, a person usually feels more alert, less fatigued and has a greater sense of well-being.

> "The closest thing to a 'magic bullet' for maintaining youth and optimal health is a well-balanced combination of exercise and proper nutrition."
>
> —*James F. Balch M.D. and Phyllis A. Balch, C.N.C.,* Prescription for Nutritional Healing

To understand the importance of exercise, we need only to look back in time. Over the centuries, people have had to work hard just to survive. To obtain food, they had to gather, grow or hunt. Meal preparation also took hard manual labor. Food was processed at home with crude tools. Bread was kneaded by hand (if you've ever done it, you know how much exercise it gives the upper body). Likewise, homes were often built by the families who lived in them. Trees had to be leveled, rough planks hewn, the frame constructed, holes dug, etc.

And think about transportation. Though there were horses and wagons and chariots, the main means of transportation was walking.

Today, we travel in air-conditioned cars to the air-conditioned supermarket to buy prepackaged meals we bring home and pop into our microwave ovens. If we make bread, we use an amazing bread machine that swallows all the ingredients and does all the kneading, punching and baking to produce a beautiful loaf.

The problem with modern conveniences and decreased manual labor is that we have also lost the benefits of exercise that were part of the labor process. *Losing these benefits has taken away the healthy strain on our hearts, muscles and bones that our bodies need.* And without exercise, our hearts become more easily diseased, our muscles atrophy and our bones thin.

The Bible and Exercise

Though there are no commandments in Scripture to do aerobic exercise three times a week, there are plenty of examples of people who did hard physical labor as well as inferences about people exerting themselves physically.

Adam was put in the garden of Eden *to work it and take*

care of it. This was before the fall of man when sin entered the world. The work was definitely made harder after sin came, but the benefits of work and exercise to the human body existed in the original world God created. After Elijah demonstrated to the prophets of Baal that *The Lord – He is God!* on Mt. Carmel, he became the first recorded marathon runner. He ran approximately 25 miles from Mt. Carmel to Jezreel, overtaking King Ahab who had left earlier in his chariot!

In Old Testament times, military training was essential for the Israelite army. David records in Psalm 18: *It is God who arms me with strength and makes my way perfect. He makes my feet like the feet of a deer; he enables me to stand on the heights. He trains my hands for battle; my arms can bend a bow of bronze.* It takes great strength to bend such a bow.

Jesus' earthly father, Joseph, was a carpenter, and we can assume that he trained Jesus as a carpenter too. This of course, was in the days before power tools. Even today, carpentry is still hard work. I recently helped a friend put on a new roof. One day was all I could take. I was sore for days afterward – and gained a new appreciation for Jesus, the carpenter.

Not only did Jesus do strengthening exercise through carpentry, but He did aerobic exercise as well. Scripture records that He traveled from town to town with His disciples during His three years of ministry. They did not take the subway. He and His companions were poor and walking was their only means of travel. From journeys recorded in the Gospels, we can presume that Jesus walked 50 miles on one particular day and 120 miles in three days on another occasion.

Paul was no wimp either. Like Christ, he did a huge amount of walking on his three missionary journeys. As a first century tentmaker, he needed to be strong. They did not have the lightweight synthetic tents in those days. Peter, Andrew, James and John were fishermen, with strength to handle heavy loads of fish in nets and row their boats through Galilean storms. The list could go on, but you get the picture. God designed our bodies to be active, and Scripture is full of godly men and women who were strong and fit to serve Him.

An Abundance of Benefits

So what are the benefits of regular physical exercise? We have already mentioned two benefits in earlier chapters: improved sleep (Eccl. 5:12a) and the relief of stress. These alone would make it worthwhile to incorporate regular exercise into your life. But exercise offers so much more. Other psychological benefits include increased creativity, self-confidence, and concentration.

> "If exercise benefits the body, it can do wonders for the mind."
> —*Kenneth Cooper, M.D.*

Medical literature is bursting with studies describing the physical benefits of exercise, and it is growing daily. There are hardly any chronic conditions that could not benefit from regular exercise. It can help obese people lose weight, hypertensives lower their blood pressure, and diabetics reduce body fat and blood sugar levels. It can help osteoporosis, improve some cancers, and help prevent heart attacks and cut the risk of stroke in half. It can lower the bad cholesterol and raise the good. It can help digestion and elimination. In the elderly, it also can prevent muscle loss, improve self-care capability and independence, and appears to prevent the "normal" deterioration of the immune function.

The spiritual benefits are harder to quantify, but the overall improvement in well-being and physical alertness can spill over to a heightened spiritual discernment and sensitivity.

Exercise and Longevity

In 1996, the "Aerobics Center Longitudinal Study" published in the *Journal of the American Medical Association* found that a low fitness level may be as great a risk to health as smoking and a greater risk than obesity, hypertension or elevated cholesterol. When they compared otherwise healthy, sedentary, non-smokers to moderately physically-fit smokers who had high blood pressure, high cholesterol or obesity, the active smokers lived longer.[41]

> "Any exercise is better than no exercise, even if it is a walk of only ten steps."
> —*Richard A. Swenson M.D.*
> *in* Margin

Two other studies give additional insight into how much exercise is needed. The first one conducted by Dr. Steven Blair was also reported in *JAMA*. The 13,000 participants were divided into five fitness categories based on treadmill testing. These ranged from Group 1 who were sedentary to Group 5 who ran 30-40 miles a week. After following them for eight years, they found that though the most fit (Group 5) had the lowest death rate, most of the benefits of exercise came between Group 1 and Group 2. In other words, by walking 30 minutes a day (the activity level of Group 2), the death rate dropped 50 to 60 percent from all causes![42]

The second study directed by Dr. Arthur S. Leon was called the Multiple Risk Factor Intervention Trial. It had over 12,000 participants who were divided into only three groups based on fitness testing. Their results were more modest – the moderate exercise group had one-third fewer deaths – but were nonetheless substantial. Plus, their definition of moderate exercise was less strict – including 30 minutes a day of walking, gardening or home repairs.[43]

In both studies, moving to a higher fitness level brought a lower death rate, but the improvement was marginal. Having balance is the key. Knowing you don't have to be a marathon runner to obtain great benefit is encouraging.

In Dr. Dean Ornish's book, *Reversing Heart Disease*, he distinguishes the difference between fitness and health. Someone can be fit through regular exercise but not be healthy. He gives examples of well-known athletes who died prematurely – some while actively participating in aerobic exercise. Jim Foxx, author of *The Complete Book of Running*, died while running. Pete Maravich, former NBA great, died playing basketball with Dr. James Dobson and other friends. Tony Conigliaro, former star of the Boston Red Sox, had a massive heart attack at age 37.[44]

Though exercise can make you fit, it is only one preventive health principle that needs to be incorporated into your total body-temple rebuilding program. Neglecting the other principles – not resting properly, not eating right, not dealing with stress appropriately – can keep us from obtaining the "Wholey Health" God wants us to experience.

Recommendations

Since the Bible does not give specific recommendations regarding exercise and physical activity, let's look at what the medical profession says about this. The following is a quote from the National Institutes of Health Consensus Conference entitled "Physical Activity and Cardiovascular Health," published in the *Journal of the American Medical Association* (JAMA), July 17, 1996:

> *All Americans should engage in regular physical activity at a level appropriate to their capacity, needs, and interest. Children and adults alike should set a goal of accumulating at least 30 minutes of moderate-intensity physical activity on most, and preferably all, days of the week.*

The article goes on to explain that the 30 minutes does not have to be done all at one time. "Intermittent or shorter bouts of activity" (of at least 10 minutes) could be used to accumulate the 30 minutes.

> "Similarly, if anyone competes as an athlete, he does not receive the victor's crown unless he competes according to the rules."
> —2 Timothy 2:5

Anyone starting from a sedentary or minimally active lifestyle should slowly build up to the recommended time period. A medical evaluation is recommended for anyone with known cardiovascular disease or for males over 40 or females over 50 with two or more cardiac risk factors (high blood pressure, obesity, smoker, elevated cholesterol, family history of heart disease). If you aren't sure, have your family physician check you over.

To be complete, your exercise program should not only include aerobic exercise, but also stretching and strengthening exercises. Let's look closer at each of these types.

Aerobic – This is the process of exercising the heart so it is beating at a target heart rate (determined by age) for at least 10 minutes at a time. Aerobic exercises include walking, bicycling, jogging, swimming, jumping rope, rebounding on a mini-tramp, hiking, racquetball, tennis, aerobics classes, dancing, cross-country skiing, rowing or similar exercises using home exercise equipment like Nordictrac or Cardioglide.

President Thomas Jefferson once said, *The sovereign invigorator of the body is exercise, and of all the exercise, walking is the best.* Listed below are some reasons why I tend to agree.

Major Benefits of Walking

1. It is safe – it causes very few injuries.
2. It is natural – we already know how.
3. It is cheap – all you need is a good pair of walking shoes.
4. It is easy – there are no particular rules.
5. It is noncompetitive.
6. It slows you down and calms your pace of life.
7. It brings you in touch with nature or your neighborhood.
8. It can be combined with other sports like golf or hiking.
9. It is flexible. It can be done anywhere, anytime, alone or with friends and at any age.
10. It is much less boring than stationary biking or other home exercise use.

My wife and I have found walking together to be a great time for us to talk. I know another couple who spend most of their time praying as they walk. But if walking does not interest you, find another aerobic activity that does. If it's not fun, you won't keep doing it.

Instead of trying to walk or swim or jog a certain distance, make your goal to keep your heart rate at the lower part of your target rate for 10-30 minutes. If you can't carry on a conversation, you have probably passed this target area. Adjust the exercise pace accordingly. Start slowly and build up. If all you can do is walk to the mailbox and back once a day, then do that for a week and then increase your distance. If you need to start even slower, that's OK too. It's more important (and safer) to start realistically and slowly than to go full throttle initially and quickly burn out. As you become more fit, you will begin to realize it will take a slightly faster pace to hit your target heart rate.

TARGET HEART RATE

Age	*Heart Rate*	*Age*	*Heart Rate*
20	120-170	45	105-150
25	120-165	50	100-145
30	115-160	55	100-140
35	110-160	60	100-135
40	110-155	65	95-130

Stretching – Besides exercising your heart, it is important to keep your body flexible. As we get older, the connective tissues in our joints, ligaments and tendons shorten and stiffen. Stretching can help lengthen the tissues and restore flexibility. Stretching can also help you avoid muscle strains and pulls. When you exercise, you are stretching your muscles beyond the usual nonexercising length. There is a danger of strain if the muscle cannot easily meet the demand for more length or more force. Stretching can prevent this strain.

I recommend 10 minutes of stretching three or more times a week. Here are some guidelines:

1. Stretch until you feel a slight pull or tension in your muscles, not to the point of pain.
2. Hold the stretch for 5-15 seconds if possible.
3. Do not bounce, but stretch gently and slowly.
4. If you work at a desk or computer for extended periods, stretching can be quite useful if done once or twice during the day.
5. Unlike aerobics, stretching exercises are a great thing to do before bed and can enhance sleep.

Here are some suggested stretching exercises that will get you started. These would be great to start your day, used as warm-up exercises before doing aerobic activities, or as a before-bedtime routine to help you relax. Start out slowly and do not force anything that feels uncomfortable. Though your flexibility should slowly increase as you exercise, you still may not improve to the point where you are stretching as far as the description or illustration indicates. Don't be concerned. Remember to keep breathing while you do these stretches. The first two exercises are good warm-up stretches.

Stretching Exercises

Neck stretch

- Start by sitting comfortably with your arms relaxed.
- Flex your neck forward so your chin moves toward your chest. Hold this for about 5-10 seconds.

- Return slowly to your starting position.
- Now extend your neck lifting your chin as far up as it will comfortably go. Hold this for 5-10 seconds, then relax.
- Then move your right ear toward your right shoulder without moving your shoulder. Hold for 5-10 seconds, then relax.
- Last, move your left ear toward your left shoulder. Hold, then relax.
- Repeat the cycle – flex, extend, right lateral flexion, left lateral flexion once or twice.

Flex stretch

- Start by lying on your back with your arms extended straight out to the side.
- Bend first one knee and then the other bringing the knees up toward your chest.
- Rotate your trunk moving both knees toward the left as far as you can comfortably go, keeping your arms extended and your upper back on the floor.
- Hold for 10-15 seconds, then relax, returning to your starting position.
- Now repeat rotating toward the right. Hold, then relax.
- Repeat one or two times.

Full body stretch

- Start by lying on the floor on your back.
- Raise your arms above your head.
- Stretch by reaching with your arms and fingers extended

and stretching your legs with your heels pointed away from you and your feet flexed toward you.
- Hold for 5-10 seconds. Remember to breathe. Relax.
- Repeat one or two times.

Leg crossover stretch

- Start by lying on your back on the floor with your arms extended out.

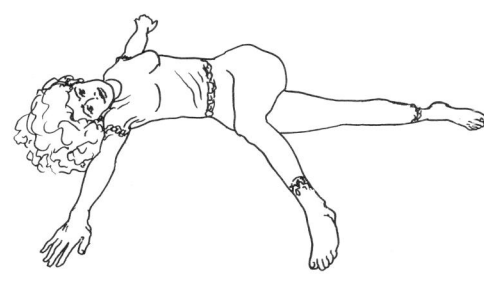

- Take your right leg and cross over stretching it toward your left hand. Keep your other arm extended and touching the floor.
- Hold for 5-15 seconds. Keep breathing. Slowly move to the starting position.
- Take your left leg and cross over stretching it toward your right hand. Hold for 5-15 seconds.
- Repeat one to three times per leg.

Side stretch

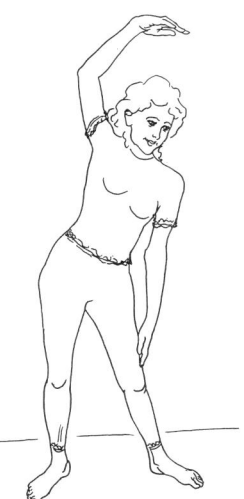

- Stand in a relaxed position.
- With your right hand reach as far down the outside of your right leg as you bend laterally at the waist.
- Extend your left arm above your head.
- Hold for 5-15 seconds, then return to standing position.
- Do the same with the opposite hand.
- Repeat 3-5 times for each side.

Towel stretch

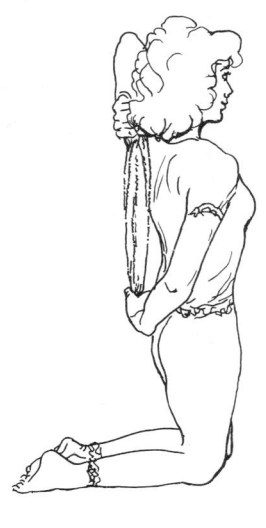

- For this one you need a rolled-up dish towel.
- Stand or sit in a comfortable position.
- Holding the towel with your right hand, reach over your right shoulder so the towel is hanging near the middle of your back.
- Reach up from behind your back with your left hand and grab the towel.
- Pull gently with both arms and hold for 5-15 seconds. Release and return to the relaxed position.
- Take the towel with the left hand now and reach over your left shoulder so the towel is hanging near the middle of your back.
- Reach up with your right hand and grab the towel.
- Pull gently as before and hold for 5-15 seconds. Release.
- Repeat for both sides one or two times.

Sitting leg stretch

- Sit with the right leg straightened in front of you and left leg pulled toward your right thigh.
- Stretch out both hands toward your right foot and hold for 10-15 seconds. Then relax.
- Switch legs so your left leg is straight and the right is pulled in and repeat the stretch.
- Repeat one or two times with each leg.

Butterfly stretch

- Sit comfortably.
- Bend both knees and pull both feet together in front of you.
- As you hold your feet with your hands, move your knees up and down like a butterfly, holding them in the extreme positions for 5-10 seconds each.
- The last time you move them down, release your hands and gently push your knees down stretching your groin muscles.
- Relax.

Balance pose stretch

- Stand comfortably near a wall or table.
- Begin by balancing on your left foot and stretching out your right arm in front of you.
- Reaching behind you with your left hand, grab your right ankle and raise it.
- Hold the pose for 10-15 seconds.
- If you have difficulty balancing, touch a wall or table with your outstretched hand.
- Return to the standing position.
- Repeat switching sides.
- Repeat one to two times for each leg.

Lower back stretch

- Start by lying comfortably on your back.
- Bending the knee, pull the right leg up against your chest and

hold for 10-15 seconds.
- Relax.
- Do the same with the left leg.
- Repeat 2-3 times for each leg.
- Then pull both knees up and hold for 10-15 seconds. Relax.

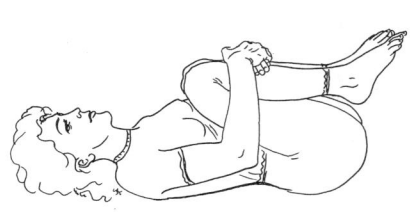

Calf stretch

- Stand about an arm's length away from a wall.
- Extend both arms in front of you so you can press your palms against the wall.
- Move your left foot back one step and bend your right knee.
- Keeping your left heel on the ground, stretch your left calf as you push against the wall. Don't force it. Hold for 5-15 seconds.
- Relax and return to the starting position.
- Now do the same thing with the right leg.

Strengthening – Strengthening or weight training exercises are not just for bodybuilders. Using calisthenics (such as pushups or situps) or dumbbells, anyone can help strengthen selected muscle groups. Nursing home patients in their 90s, who were started on light weights, improved their strength and became increasingly more active. When people combine aerobic exercise with weight training, it results in greater bone density than if aerobic exercise is done solely. This is important for menopausal women since they are at risk for osteoporosis.

I recommend about 10-15 minutes of weight training exercises three times a week. Here are some examples of strengthening exercises you may want to use to get started. Most of the exercises are familiar calisthenics. A few require the use of a pair of dumbbells (marked by an asterisk *) that should weigh about 2 1/2 to 5 pounds each. You can easily get by without these, but they do give you more options.

One reason I like these exercises is you can do them at home without going to a gym. Some people might prefer a gym membership with its access to weights and equipment. Find out what works best for you.

It is important to go slowly and build up. If your workout is easy, you can always do more repetitions next time. But if it is too difficult, you might injure yourself in the process. If there is a modified version of the exercise described, begin with that for the first week or two at least. Also, it is suggested the exercises with weights be added after doing the less strenuous calisthenics for the first few weeks. Later, adding a second set to each exercise will also increase the difficulty of the workout.

One more thing. Check your pulse during your strengthening exercise routine. If you are in your target heart rate, you can also count this time as part of your aerobic workout.

Strengthening Exercises

Push-ups (Modified)

- Lying on your abdomen, place the palms of your hands at shoulder level on the ground.

- Keeping your knees on the ground, push off with your arms, raising your body until your arms are extended.
- Return to within 4-6 inches of the ground by bending your elbows.
- This is one cycle. Do 5 to 30 cycles.

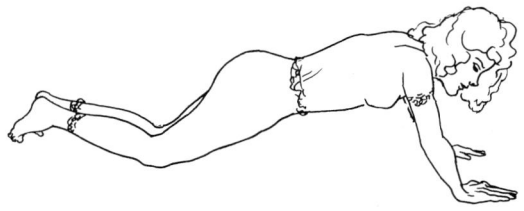

Push-ups (Standard)

- Same as above except use your toes instead of your knees.
- Remember to breathe.

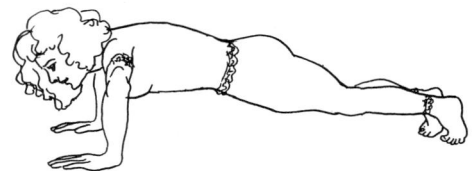

Seat drop

- Sit on the edge of an armless chair with your legs stretched out straight in front of you.
- Place your hands on the front edge and hold yourself up with your arms as you move your buttocks off the seat.
- Now use your arms to lower your seat and raise it. (One cycle.)

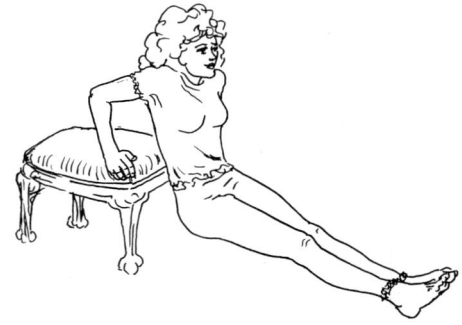

- Do not allow your elbows to flex greater than 90 degrees.
- Do 2 to 12 cycles.

*Lying bench press**

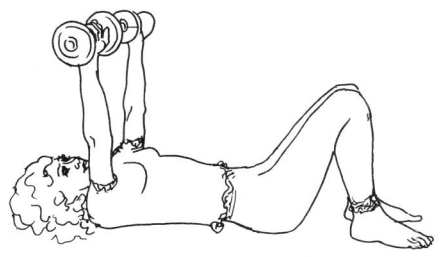

- Lie on the floor or a bench on your back.
- Using dumbbells at shoulder level, raise them up above your chest extending your arms, then lower them. (One cycle.)
- Continue for 10 to 20 cycles.

Modified sit-up (abdominal crunch)

- Lie on the floor on your back with your knees bent and your lower legs resting comfortably on a chair or couch.
- With your arms crossed in front of your chest, and chin on chest, raise your shoulders off the floor (no more than 45 degrees) for a count of one. Then slowly lower yourself back down. (One cycle.)
- Continue for 10 to 20 cycles.

Weighted sit-up*

- This is identical to the modified sit-up except you will be holding dumbbells with your hands to give more resistance.
- Do 10 to 20 cycles.

Lateral leg lifts

- Lie on one side propped with your underside elbow.
- Using your upper leg, lift it straight up laterally away from your body. Return to original position. (One cycle.)
- Continue for 10 to 30 cycles.
- Repeat using the opposite leg.

Posterior leg lifts

- Get in a 'baby crawl' position on your knees and elbows.
- Starting with one leg, lift it above the floor as far as is comfortable, keeping the knee bent toward the ceiling, then return. (One cycle.)
- Continue for 10 to 30 cycles, then do the opposite leg.

Forward lunge

- Stand comfortably with arms extended like wings.
- Starting with your right leg step forward and bend your knee but do not bend it greater than 90 degrees (keep your back as straight as possible).
- Return to original position.
- Do the same with your left leg and return. (One cycle includes both leg movements.)

- Continue for 10 to 20 cycles. (Start slowly with this one.)
- *With weights, hold them down at your sides.

Calf raise

- Stand comfortably.
- Rise up on your toes, then return. (One cycle.)
- Continue for 10 to 30 cycles.
- *With weights, hold them down at your sides.

> "Everyone who competes in the games goes into strict training. They do it to get a crown that will not last; but we do it to get a crown that will last forever."
>
> —*1 Corinthians 9:25*

In summary, start slowly and build up. Choose exercises that you enjoy. Find a friend or exercise partner to help you stay committed. Give priority to the aerobic form; it is the most important to your overall health. For added benefits, begin to incorporate stretching and strengthening exercises as well. Worthy goals for each form would be:

Aerobic – 30 minutes 3-6 times per week
Stretching – 10 minutes 3 times per week
Strengthening – 10 to 15 minutes 3 times per week*

Schedule it into your week. Pray for the Lord's strength. Concentrate on the sustained target heart rate over a period of time rather than distance. Slow down and rest when you need to. Listen to your body. Warm up before and cool down afterwards so the heart gradually goes faster and gradually comes back down to normal. Keep your perspective. As 1 Timothy 4:8 says, *For physical training is of some value, but godliness has value for all things, holding promise for both the present life and the life to come.*

A Word About Excuses

One comment I often hear from patients when I bring up the subject of exercise is that they already get plenty of

---

* Strengthening exercises may count for aerobic also, so check your pulse.

exercise during the day in their daily activities. One woman says she is constantly on the go as she watches young children. A man says he is always on his feet as he walks up and down the factory floor.

This kind of activity has some benefit and is much better than being sedentary. But to get true aerobic benefit to your heart, the activity must raise your heart rate into the target range for a sustained amount of time (at least 10 minutes). Next time you're doing that activity, check your pulse and see if you're in the target range. If so, time how long it stays there.

Another common excuse is that patients don't have the energy to start exercising. It is difficult to convince them that by getting up off the couch and walking the dog or exercising to an aerobics tape, their energy will actually increase. It is a matter of overcoming the inertia. I have come home from work exhausted, wanting to zone out in front of the TV. My wife will often convince me to go with her for a walk and it never fails to make me feel better.

The third most common excuse has to do with time – or lack of it. Where can you fit 30 minutes of exercise into an already busy schedule? When you make it a priority, it can be done. For many, cutting out 30 minutes of TV may be the key. Using part of your lunch hour at work is another possibility. Getting up a half-hour earlier and exercising is a great way to get your day started. Be creative. Seek God's help and strength.

Spiritual Connection – Running Hard After Jesus

The Christian life is an exercise in faith. Aerobically, we need to *run in such a way as to get the prize* following *in His steps*. We need to utilize our spiritual muscles and *be strong in the Lord* and *fight the good fight*. And we need to stretch and *press on toward the goal*, reaching for God's higher purposes and our higher calling.

We have the master trainer at our side, coaching us at every step. And the race we're running has already been won!

Recommended Reading:

Cooper, Kenneth. *Faith-Based Fitness*. Nashville: Thomas Nelson, 1997.

Schlosberg, Suzanne and Liz Neporent. *Fitness for Dummies*. IDG Books Worldwide, 1996.

Bailey, Covert. *The New Fit or Fat*. Houghton Mifflin Co., 1991.

CHAPTER FIVE

The Blessings of Self-Control

A few months ago, the ABC newsmagazine program 20/20 aired its annual segment on the Dilley sextuplets. We received an upclose and personal update on the lives of the six six-year-olds as Diane Sawyer reported after visiting in their home.

The Dilleys are a lively, healthy, noisy bunch and we saw glimpses into their rambunctious play and conversation. One part of the broadcast especially interested me, as the six children were tested for self-control. They placed one child at a time in a room alone, sitting at a table with a plate containing four M & Ms. The children were told that the adult would be leaving the room for 12 minutes and that if they could wait to eat the M & Ms, they would be rewarded with four more pieces. A hidden camera showed how each coped with this temptation – singing, sitting on hands, counting, or talking. 20/20 reported that a third of all six-year-olds are not able to successfully wait out the 12 minutes and instead eat the candy. Interestingly, all six Dilley children were successful in this self-control exercise!

What was it that enabled these children to wait? What is their secret to self-control? Or is there a secret?

These are, of course, vital questions. Everywhere we look today we see evidence of a society lacking self-control, whether it is in the area of food intake, substance abuse, sexual sin, or criminal violence. We see it in our leaders whether in government or in business. We see it in secular organizations and in our churches. We see it in others and we see it when we look in the mirror.

Self-control is crucial to many areas of life, including the practice of preventive health principles. We need self-control to keep the Sabbath and choose to rest. We need self-control to seek the peace of God, to make healthy food choices, and to exercise. We need self-control for both proactive "doing the right thing" activities, as well as the "not doing the wrong thing" activities, such as smoking, addictive behaviors, gluttony and sexual sin.

Both types of self-control require a decision to say either yes or no. To keep the Sabbath, we are saying no to time pressures and yes to God's healing rest. When we avoid tobacco, we are saying no to peer pressure and our unhealthy attempts to satisfy needs, and yes to health and pure air. For people recovering from substance abuse, addiction or dysfunctional family issues, learning to say no is essential. In *Days of Healing, Days of Joy,* authors Earnie Larson and Carol Larson Hegarty affirm the importance of this discipline:

Actually, joy is the freedom to do what needs to be done. And gaining that freedom takes discipline.... It takes discipline to say no when we need to – when every fiber of our being may be urging us to give in again. It takes discipline to stand up and be counted when our pattern has been to fade into the wallpaper and blend in with any situation.[45]

> "Learn to say no; it will be of more use to you than to be able to speak Latin."
> —Charles Spurgeon

Nevertheless, when the subject of self-control comes up, most people react as if it were a dirty word. There are images of legalism, *thou shalt nots*, and the guilt almost everyone feels because of personal areas lacking discipline. Self-control is not about perfectionism, however, but about gradually developing maturity. It is about setting boundaries for your life. Healthy boundaries. It is about taking some responsible for your life and health. Self-control is about self-love and self-worth – loving yourself enough to care for your body.

The Costs of Self-Control

Self-control centers on making choices – choosing things that bring health and rejecting things that bring death. It acknowledges that we are not victims of fate or circumstances. God has given us power to do something about our life – our physical life, our emotional life, and our spiritual life.

These choices can be costly. If we have no boundaries, we reap a society smitten with abuse, chaos, and confusion. But choosing the path of self-control also has its price tag. *Self control always costs something in the short-term, but the long-term rewards are well worth it – both for us and society.*

> "Like a city whose walls are broken down is a man who lacks self-control."
> —*Proverbs 25:28*

The cost of sacrifice

When Israel's King Solomon began to build the temple, he knew it would involve a huge sacrifice of money and time, but he was willing to pay whatever it cost (1 Kings 5:6). He had to direct workers away from other projects so the temple could be built, and it took seven full years to complete!

Sometimes a patient who has recently been diagnosed with a chronic condition (such as diabetes, hypertension or heart disease) will say to me, "Listen, Doc, this is my wake-up call. I don't want to take medication for the rest of my life. I will do anything it takes to get my body back in shape, even if it means eating cardboard." Then I want to shout, "Alright!!" I know these patients are going to be successful, because they are willing to make the big sacrifices to improve their health.

When someone realizes that the answer to their health problem is not found in a pill or some other quick fix, they are miles down the road to recovery. Real solutions take time and involve several aspects of life. In the fall 1996 issue of *Biomedical Inquiry*, H.L. Mencken is quoted as saying, *For every complex problem there is a solution that is simple, direct, and wrong.*[46]

In the Crown Ministries Bible Study, students are taught that God owns everything, and we are just stewards of His finances. The same is true of our physical bodies. We are not our own. Our bodies belong to the Lord, and we are simply stewards of His temple. We cannot abdicate our responsibility saying, "God will take care of me." If we neglect God's disciplines, the body becomes more susceptible to disease and premature death. Author Stormie Omartian says, *Remember, no one is invincible or above God's laws. Please care enough about God, yourself, and those who love you, to change your ways.*[47]

The cost of delayed gratification

One sign of maturity in children is their willingness to accept delayed gratification. M. Scott Peck, in his popular book entitled *The Road Less Traveled*, defines delaying gratification as *a process of scheduling the pain and pleasure of life in such a way as to enhance the pleasure by meeting and experiencing the pain first and getting it over with.* Even adults struggle with this process.

These principles of health have a lot to do with delayed gratification. By going through the pain of regular exercise now, we later experience the health benefits of a stronger heart and more flexible body. By going through the pain of fasting, we later experience the health benefits of a cleansed body. By going through the pain (at first) of not eating junk food, we later experience health benefits which may include less frequent headaches, improved digestion, and less chance of obesity. By going through the pain of slowing down and resting (which can be a pain to some people), we later experience the health benefits of increased energy and mental acuity. Most things worth doing involve some discipline, pain, or a putting off of the reward.

The cost of discipline

In our comfort-oriented society we tend to avoid pain at all costs. But to mature spiritually, we must endure discipline. Hebrews 12:11 says, *No discipline seems pleasant at the time, but painful. Later on, however, it produces a harvest of righteousness and peace for those who have been trained by it.*

Jesus Himself said, *If anyone would come after me, he must deny himself and take up his cross and follow me. For whoever wants to save his life will lose it, but whoever loses his life for me will find it* (Matt. 16:24,25).

Jesus exemplifies the disciplined life. In His first temptation in the wilderness, after fasting for forty days, Satan tempts Him to satisfy His physical hunger. Jesus says no to Satan and yes to the voice of God. This example shows us the connection between physical desires being brought under submission and spiritual desires following suit.

The supreme example is Jesus dying on the cross, surrendering His will to Father God. Putting God's plans ahead of self caused the ultimate pain and a cruel death, but provided salvation for all and a resurrected, glorified body.

> "As far as your self-control goes,
> as far goes your freedom."
> —*Marie von Ebner-Eschenbach*

The danger of self-righteousness

A man walked into the doctor's office and said, "Doctor, I have this awful headache that never leaves me. Could you give me something for it?"

"I will," said the doctor, "but I want to check a few things out first. Tell me, do you drink a lot of liquor?"

"Liquor?" said the man indignantly. "I never touch the filthy stuff."

"How about smoking?"

"I think smoking is disgusting. I've never in my life touched tobacco."

"I'm a bit embarrassed to ask this, but – you know the way some men are – do you do any running around at night?"

"Of course not. What do you take me for? I'm in bed every night by ten o'clock at the latest."

"Tell me," said the doctor, "the pain in the head you speak of, is it a sharp, shooting kind of pain?"

"Yes," said the man. "That's it – a sharp, shooting kind of pain."

"Simple, my dear fellow! Your trouble is you have your halo on too tight. All we need to do is loosen it a bit."[48]

When we start to address self-control in our life, we face the enormous risk of creating a bigger monster than the areas that are out of control. That monster is self-righteousness. If there was one thing Jesus hated, it was self-righteousness. Just read what He said to the Pharisees in Matthew 23. Paul gets pretty hot also when he writes to the Galatians that salvation is by faith in Christ, and not by observing the law.

So how do we deal with the issue of self-control? Or, more generally, how do we deal with any of these preventive health principles without them becoming intertwined into a spirit of religiosity?

Being honest helps. In Romans 7, Paul describes a process that most of us can identify with:

I do not understand what I do. For what I want to do I do not do, but what I hate I do.... For I have the desire to do what is good, but I cannot carry it out.... So I find this law at work: When I want to do good, evil is right there with me.... What a wretched man I am! Who will rescue me from this body of death? Thanks be to God – through Jesus Christ our Lord!

It is obvious we need more than self to be successful in self-control. We need help from God through Jesus Christ. We need His strength, patience, forgiveness and many times, healing from past hurts. And more than anything else, we need His love.

Self-control and a father's love

In John and Paula Sandford's book, *Restoring the Christian Family*, there is a chapter entitled, "The Importance of a Father's Love." In it they discuss a prison ministry called "The Vision," headed by a man named Carl Foss. Mr. Foss calls for men to be father-substitutes to prisoners on a one-on-one basis. The reasoning: over 90% of prisoners have never known the love of a father. To illustrate his point, Foss relates a story that occurred at a prison on McNeil Island. There, one of the prisoners who was a gifted artist had designed a handmade Father's Day card which he initially offered for sale to his fellow inmates. He got no takers even when he reduced the price by 50%, nor when he tried to give it away. No one wanted the card. Not one of the 1,280 prisoners had a father who they wanted to honor by sending a Father's Day card.[49]

Not everyone who lacked fathering becomes a criminal, but to whatever extent we didn't have loving parental mirrors, to that measure we fail to see ourselves clearly. If we haven't been loved, accepted, or disciplined adequately, we tend to not be in touch with who we are or know what we want or need. And instead of operating out of whom we were created to be, we tend to react to people, either by rebelling and fighting against authority, or by unhealthy pleasing and trying to earn our worth as a person or our place in the universe. If we were denied our basic longings for appropriate love, acceptance, and boundaries, we desperately attempted to parent ourselves and make sense and order of our lives. As we grew, this may have become overcontrol, as we attempted to make ourselves acceptable. We cannot make ourselves better by our own efforts alone, however, so instead we tried to at least act better, to hide and deny our darknesses. So we became hypocrites, clinging to an image of ourselves that was not true or life-giving. Often our churches, in trying to make us good, instead made us liars or pretenders, or if we couldn't fake it, failures.

But if we are loved, it's another story. True self-control is a natural flow out of being loved and gently guided. We can only make good decisions for "self" when that self has been loved and thus awakened to life and truth. God doesn't just make us and be done with it. No, we start out with a gene pool and certain predispositions. Then we need to be nurtured for 18 years and to have who we are discovered, encouraged, and actually called into being.[50]

Don't despair; all of us had imperfect parents to some extent. As adults we have options, such as receiving nurture in the body of Christ or learning to parent ourselves in a healthier way through therapy and other means. It's true what they say in some 12 Step groups, "It's never too late to have a happy childhood." This is especially possible with our heavenly Father, who called all things into being and is able and longing to bring us into full life. As we begin to let into our hearts the magnitude of acceptance by Love Himself, we grow in awareness of who God is and He shows us who we are. Then we can begin to let go and trust Him with life. It's ironic that life and self-control begin with letting go of control and allowing ourselves to be loved.

Brennan Manning, author of *The Ragamuffin Gospel*, states:

> *Over the years, the growing consciousness of radical grace has wrought profound changes in my self-awareness. Justification by grace through faith means that I know myself accepted by God as I am. When my head is enlightened and my heart is pierced by this truth, I can accept myself as I am.* **Genuine self-acceptance is... an act of faith in the God of grace.**
>
> *Several times in my ministry people have expressed the fear that self-acceptance will abort the ongoing conversion process and lead to a life of spiritual laziness and moral laxity. Nothing could be more untrue. The acceptance of self does not mean to be resigned to the status quo. On the contrary, the more fully we accept ourselves, the more successfully we begin to grow. Love is a far better stimulus than threat or pressure.*[51]

Look at the progression in 2 Peter 1:5-7. It says,

> *For this very reason, make every effort to add to your faith goodness; and to goodness, knowledge; and to knowledge, self-control; and to self-control, perseverance; and to perseverance, godliness; and to godliness, brotherly kindness; and to brotherly kindness, love.*

The beginning point here is not self-control. Nor is it knowledge, for even when we know we are doing unhealthy things to our bodies, it doesn't usually motivate us to stop. No, after being touched by God's love, our first response is faith, believing in the God who is. This God loves and parents us and celebrates our every victory and doesn't focus on our failures. He doesn't expect us to know what we haven't yet learned. He doesn't shame us for mistakes, but delights in slowly and patiently bringing us to maturity. He even partners with us in straightening out our health and gives us the strength to be good to our body-temples.*

Larry Briney, one of my former pastors, wrote a terrific little article a few years ago entitled *Cause and Effect!* that illustrates my point. He writes:

> *We spend way too much time fighting effects when our time, energies, money, and prayers would be more fruitful if directed at causes. Herein lies wisdom: to discern one from the other.... Self-control is an effect caused by the rule of King Jesus in my life.*[52]

This idea is the basis for this entire study. Why treat disease and sickness when we can get to the cause and prevent them? Living a Christ-centered life encourages our making life-giving choices. In Galatians 5, the apostle Paul describes self-control as a fruit of the Spirit. Fruits are not manufactured. Fruits are natural products that occur when a tree is nurtured with the essentials of life. When we allow ourselves to be soaked in the Father's love, faith begins to grow, and His Holy Spirit begins to produce the fruit of love, joy, peace, patience, and self-control.

I think that is the secret to how the Dilly sextuplets kept from eating the M & Ms. They were secure in the love and discipline they received from their parents, and it produced the fruit of self-control.

---

* Though Scripture primarily presents God as our Father, God also uses metaphors of mothering to describe His love for His people (see Deut. 32:11; Isa. 66:13; Matt. 23:37). Picturing this feminine side of God can be very helpful to some people, especially victims of abuse or those lacking adequate mothering.

Now let's look at specific activities that call for self-control.

Fasting for Better Spiritual and Physical Health

Having self-control to start a food program is one thing. Having self-control to go without food is quite another. While the discipline of exercise gives almost immediate rewards (more strength and flexibility and a greater sense of well-being), fasting seems only to produce weakness and hunger.

No one can say for sure how prevalent the discipline of fasting is today in the modern church because it's a private matter between the believer and the Lord. Jesus instructed us to *do it in secret* and the subject is rarely spoken of in most churches. Consider how long it's been since you last heard a sermon about fasting or read a book on the subject. In Arthur Wallis' book *God's Chosen Fast*, written in 1968, he described this Christian discipline as "out of vogue." Thirty years later, I'm not sure its place in most Christians' lives has changed.

Why do we neglect this principle? Perhaps it is due to ignorance about the value of fasting. Or perhaps there is a fear that it is unhealthy or that we could never do it. We may remember the few hours of misery we've felt when we skipped just one meal and wondered how we could go without several meals. Some view fasting as a hypocritical form of asceticism or legalism, but Wallis refutes this view. He says, *We do not abandon seasons of prayer or the habit of giving to God simply because the Pharisees abused these. Regular fasting need not become ritualistic, any more than regular praying.*

The Scripture notes that many of the great men and women of the Bible fasted, including Moses, David, Elijah, Daniel, Hannah, Anna, John the Baptist, and Jesus Himself.

In the "Sermon on the Mount," He introduces His teaching on this subject with the words, *When you fast...* not *If you fast....* But His followers did not fast while He was with them on earth. It was not the right time. It was time to celebrate while the bridegroom was with them. Jesus says that when the bridegroom is taken away, then they will fast.

What is a fast?

A fast is going without food for a specific length of time. In one sense, all of us fast every night when we sleep. When we get up the next morning, we break the fast with breakfast. However, fasting implies missing at least one normally scheduled meal.

There are other types of fasts which we might include as forms of self-denial. A few years ago, our church participated in a one-week media fast. No television, no radio, no newspapers. It was a wonderful discipline and God showed us much. The celebration of Lent might be considered a type of fast, when individuals decide to give up something from Ash Wednesday until Easter. Though all of these forms of self-denial can be beneficial, the purpose of this section is to discuss the Biblical injunction for us "to fast," which means primarily "not to eat."

There are a few examples in the Bible in which a fasting individual not only went without food, but also without water. These, obviously, were supernaturally guided and protected, for our bodies cannot normally survive without water more than a few days. Do not fast without drinking water.

Some good reasons for fasting

Having the right motive is a key factor in the discipline of fasting. It's important to ask yourself why you are fasting, because you can be doing the right thing for the wrong reason and miss out on the intended blessing. From the examples in Scripture, it is clear that the most important reason to fast is for the glory of God. If we fast with selfish motives, thinking that we can twist God's arm in our favor, we are misdirected. Pastor-author Jack Hayford has written, *Fasting is never earning things from God, but is for learning things from Him.*

The Scriptures show us a multitude of other good reasons to fast. Many times a fast was combined with a time of mourning in response to a personal or national tragedy, such as when Saul and Jonathan were killed in battle. Often fasting accompanied repentance when someone was confronted with personal or national sin. Nehemiah led such a fast for the exiles who had returned to Jerusalem and rebuilt the wall. Sometimes it was used as a time for intercession, to seek God's help and intervention, such as when Jehoshaphat proclaimed a fast after learning about an approaching army. Jesus fasted in preparation for His ministry. It is also a powerful tool when used in spiritual warfare, to free captives, or to break bonds of addiction or demonic possession.

A fast should draw us closer to God and align us more closely with His purposes so He is glorified.

How long to fast?

A fast could be as short as missing one meal. Jesus fasted for 40 days in the wilderness to prepare for His ministry. My recommendation is to start off slowly, missing one meal initially. Then gradually stretch that to two meals, then three meals. After you have been doing 24-hour fasts regularly for awhile, then try going to 36 hours. If you are planning to fast for longer than three days, I suggest you read one or more of the reference books on fasting listed at the end of this chapter. If you are on medication or have any significant health problems, consult your physician before beginning a fast.

The physical side of fasting

What happens physiologically to our bodies when we fast? Our body needs energy to carry out all of its many functions, from hormonal to neurologic; from muscular to thought processing. The energy currency of the body is glucose. When we stop eating, the body must switch from the dietary source of energy to body reserves. Initially, this is glucose from the liver and muscles, stored in the form of glycogen. When this reserve is depleted, the body then taps into its fat supply, converting the fats or lipids into glucose. This produces byproducts called ketones, which, after two to three days of fasting, are usually of sufficient quantity in the blood to decrease our appetites.

The typical digestive process, in which the body breaks down the food, absorbs it and transports it throughout the body, takes great energy. In fasting, just as in sleep, this process is given a rest. This allows the body to use this energy to do some housecleaning or "temple cleaning." Fasting gives the body extra time to shed the effects of the pollution and toxins we are exposed to every day. No matter how careful we are, we may ingest pesticides or herbicides in food, carbon monoxide from secondhand smoke and microorganisms in our water. Even the breakdown of fairly healthy food can create toxins in our system that need to be eliminated. The liver, lungs, kidneys, skin and bowels are the main organs of elimination, and through fasting, these organs are able to become super-cleaners within our system.

Some of the common symptoms of fasting are caused as

the body removes impurities and eliminates toxins. A coated tongue, headaches, nausea, nasal congestion and phlegm are all evidence of the body ridding itself of impurities. Other possible reactions are weakness and lightheadedness. Because the digestive process is not producing its usual amount of dissipated heat, chills are also common. Most of these reactions are mild and decrease significantly as one practices fasting on a regular basis, and combines it with a healthy diet and the other health habits mentioned in this book. If any of these become extreme or unbearable, simply go off the fast.

Who should not fast?

Some people should not fast because of medical reasons. Diabetics should not fast. Their glucose metabolism is not functioning properly and there are significant dangers that can occur when they go without food. Pregnant and nursing mothers should also not fast. Their bodies are providing nourishment for themselves and their child, and fasting is not advisable. If you have a chronic medical condition (such as hypertension, heart disease, liver or kidney disease), it is advisable that you check with your physician to see if it is safe for you to fast for a period of time.

Sometimes these same people who should avoid a complete fast because of medical problems can still participate in a juice fast in which the only oral intake besides water is fresh fruit or vegetable juices. Diabetics, especially, should still check with their physician, and if clearance is given, stick with vegetable juices (to avoid the high sugar content of fruit juices) and monitor their blood sugar several times a day.

How to break a fast

Coming off the fast is critical and probably requires more self-control than the fast itself. This is because of the tendency to "make up for lost time" and gorge yourself with food. Nothing could be worse. When we do this to our bodies, it creates a lot of unnecessary abdominal pain and overall misery that only reinforces to our flesh that we made a mistake by fasting in the first place. I know from experience that overeating after fasting is not pleasant. Go slowly. Take your time to "taste for the first time" simple foods that God has given us.

Probably the best way to come off a fast is to drink fresh fruit or vegetable juice as your first meal. This allows the stomach and digestive organs to "wake up" slowly and return to their normal digestive responsibilities. If fresh juice is not available, then fresh fruit alone works well. Other possibilities include a green salad or lightly steamed vegetables or a baked potato. Eat them plain without condiments if possible. Again, the temptation here is to overeat, so be very attuned to your stomach and stop at the first signs of fullness. Make an extra effort to eat the Eden or Daniel diet for the next few days after a fast. Avoid the high fat foods of the Egyptian/American diet. Allow what you learned on the fast to change your diet more toward what God would want you to eat. Let fresh fruits and vegetables, whole grains, seeds, nuts and pure water satisfy your body's needs. They make the best ingredients for the ongoing work of your body/temple.

> *Arthur Wallis' golden rules for breaking a fast:*
> 1. Watch your quantities
> 2. Eat slowly and masticate [chew] well
> 3. Stop at the first warning sign
> 4. Rest as much as possible
> 5. Don't try to do too much too soon

Some final recommendations

1. Prepare for the fast spiritually. Look at your motives. What is the spiritual focus God is calling you to look at during the fast?
2. *Man cannot live on bread alone*, but God's Word can sustain us with spiritual food during the fast. I like Stormie Omartian's recommendation to read Isaiah 58 during every fast.
3. Avoid broadcasting your fast to the world (Matt. 6:16,17). The support of a friend or two, however, can be a help.*
4. Prepare for the fast physically. Don't try to feast every meal for two days in anticipation. Don't launch into a fast on a sugar high from rich desserts.
5. Drink plenty of pure water.
6. If you are new to fasting, start slowly. Then gradually extend your time without food as you gain experience.
7. If you aren't able to do a complete fast, consider a juice fast.
8. Break the fast wisely.

Substance Abuse and Addiction

The latest statistics indicate we are losing the war on drugs. Marijuana, heroin, cocaine and other illegal drugs are regaining popularity among both older and younger people, with even kids in grade school becoming early

---

* God seems to be calling the church to more corporate fasting, and on these occasions, sharing your struggles or experiences can be a great source of encouragement.

addicts. Our culture clearly contributes to this growing phenomenon. Even in homes where there are no illegal drugs, parents may be addicted to alcohol, nicotine products, prescription medications, caffeine or even food.

The most common and dangerous of these "legal" addictions is cigarette smoking. Smoking has been called the number one preventable health hazard in this country. If cigarette smoking was eliminated in America, the health savings would be astronomical. It is a significant risk factor for coronary artery disease, emphysema, cancers and a host of other diseases. The number of premature deaths in this country each year attributed to smoking is over 400,000. To put that in perspective, it would be like three jumbo jets crashing every day for one year without any survivors!

> "Anyone caught smoking will be promptly hit over the head with an organic carrot."
> —*Sign seen in a Houston health food restaurant*

Alcoholism and alcohol-related diseases also take a devastating toll on society. From cirrhosis to drunken driving to neuropathy to overwhelming emotional pathology, the overuse of alcohol destroys millions of lives each year.

Caffeine may not be at the top of your list of abusable substances, but I include it because it is a stimulant that can be addictive and is often misused. It may come as a surprise that food is also on this list, but compulsive eating is an epidemic problem in this country, one that is more socially acceptable than other addictions, and therefore the "drug of choice" for many. Our indulgences in rich feast foods cause many health problems that are identified in the food chapter.

Some addictions involve behaviors rather than substances. Anything we focus on (worship) to numb our pain or keep us from facing reality can become just as toxic in our life as a heroin addiction. Workaholism and exercise can be misused in this way. In fact, we can abuse almost any "good" thing including religion or worship, if we are using it to hide our hurts.[53]

We do well to be patient with ourselves and get support as we learn healthier ways of coping that will eventually replace our addictions. There is no quick fix to these problems. The scope of this book is not intended to cover this complex subject in any great detail. However, let me give some general guidelines:

- If you identify with any of these addictions, the first step is to admit your problem. Talk to your spouse, a friend or your pastor. If appropriate, discuss it with your doctor. You may need a professional counselor, psychologist or psychiatrist. Get involved in a group. The 12-step groups that began with Alcoholics Anonymous have branched into almost every one of these addictions from narcotics to overeaters. The 12 steps work because they are biblically based.[54]

- Ask your doctor about products that can help someone quit smoking. There are several choices available now including patches, gum, prescription tablets and herbal products.

- Besides the support group, get prayer support from at least two Christian friends.

- Be extra patient with yourself; this is a huge undertaking.

> "1. We admitted we were powerless over alcohol [or insert your addiction here] – that our lives had become unmanageable.
>
> 2. Came to believe that a Power greater than ourselves could restore us to sanity.
>
> 3. Made a decision to turn our will and our lives over to the care of God as we understood Him."
>
> —*First three steps of the 12 Steps of Alcoholics Anonymous*

Sex is a Good Thing (and a God Thing)

Sexual activity is largely out of control in our society – and God hates it. But that doesn't mean He is down on sex, He's only down on the misuse of it. He created sex for developing intimacy between a husband and wife, both for procreation and pleasure. Sex, as He intended it, causes the two to become one physically, emotionally and even spiritually.

God designed our bodies in such a way that the man and woman fit together perfectly. They lie heart to heart, able to hold each other close and look into each other's eyes. There is deep fellowship, the mingling of spirits as the two "know" each other. There is the sexual release or orgasm, an intense, pleasurable feeling experienced by both sexes.

God created sex to be pleasurable. The woman's clitoris is a sensory organ that has only one purpose – to give her pleasure during lovemaking. We humans are not like animals that have periods of heat which instinctively give them the desires for sexual union. We have sexual desires even when we are not fertile.

And if you want further evidence that God intended sex for pleasure, you need only read the Song of Solomon. Some writers have called this short book of the Bible a sex manual. It describes the intense love between a man and a woman, and the consummation of that love on their wedding night.

Sex is indeed very good. God made it so. Man, however, has polluted God's good thing. With the help of Satan, he has taken that which was designed for intimacy in marriage, and distorted it by removing all boundaries. The results have been devastating. Disease, death, guilt, rape and sexual deviancy are just a few of the consequences of disregarding God's guidelines. It breaks His heart that something He created for our good could cause such pain. God wants to protect us, but all the inherent goodness of sex turns to pain and problems when His laws are broken.

Gold standards

In medicine, the term "gold standard" is used for a test or therapy that gives the absolute best result. It is the standard by which all other tests or therapies are measured. In the past, the gold standard for treatment of strep throat was penicillin. For detection of a deep venous thrombosis (blood clot), the gold standard was a venogram. As research went on, some of these gold standards changed. Some streptococcal organisms became resistant to penicillin and required newer antibiotics. Techniques in ultrasound were discovered that gave more accurate results in detecting a deep venous thrombosis and with fewer complications.

In the area of sexual behavior, God has given us, through His Word, several guidelines which I would consider "gold standards." These guidelines have never changed nor will they ever need to be updated because of new research or scientific discoveries. I believe they were true when God originally communicated these guidelines through Moses, Jesus and Paul; and they remain true today. In making choices about our sexual behavior, we should compare our choices with the "gold standards" of God's Word.

Gold Standard #1 – **Save Sex for Marriage** –
1 Thess. 4:3,4; 1 Cor. 6:18.

Gold Standard #2 – **Marriage Unites One Man and One Woman** –
Mark 10:7-9; Lev. 18:22.

Gold Standard #3 – **Remain Faithful to Your Marriage Partner** –
Exod. 20:14; Heb. 13:4.

Gold Standard #4 – **Guard Your Heart** –
Prov. 4:23; Psalm 101:3a; Matt. 5:28.

There are an increasing number of voices echoing the message of God's Word to practice abstinence (sexual self-control) until marriage. Colleen Kelly Mast is the author of *Sex Respect*, an abstinence-based sex education curriculum with the overall objective being that students *realize that true sexual freedom includes the freedom to say 'No' to sex outside of marriage.* Boston University has developed *The Art of Loving Well*, a literature-based curriculum using excellent short stories to teach character and to *guide students to see that premature sexual intimacy can bring with it severe consequences.*

> "With regard to AIDS, science and morality teach the same lesson. The Surgeon General's Report on AIDS makes it clear that the best way to avoid AIDS is a mutually faithful monogamous sexual relationship. Until it is possible to establish and maintain such a relationship, abstinence is safest."
>
> —*Statement on AIDS Education by William Bennett, Secretary of Education and C. Everett Koop, M.D., Surgeon General: Jan. 30, 1987*

When sex is saved for marriage, there are many benefits. For example, the chance of getting sexually transmitted diseases (STD) is almost nonexistent. During the dating or courtship process, there is a wonderful freedom that happens when couples don't have the pressures and distractions of a sexual relationship. In this context they can get to know one another and truly become friends. They can concentrate on sharing and communicating with each other.

When a man and woman wait until married to have sex, many painful situations are avoided, such as out-of-wedlock pregnancy. By waiting, they also build a deep level of trust and commitment, and have a greater chance for long-term success in their marriage. Recent studies also show that monogamous couples have greater sexual satisfaction than those who have sex outside marriage.

Those who have fallen short of God's standards can still experience a new dimension of sexual purity through repentance and God's grace. In Isaiah 1:18 the Lord challenges His people to do what is right and makes this promise to those who turn to Him in obedience: *Though your sins are like scarlet, they shall be as white as snow....* This Scripture is, of course, fulfilled in Jesus. On Earth He showed Himself to be the friend and companion of sinners who were loved to repentence.

The Spiritual Connection: Love and Self-Control

There are several spiritual connections already addressed in this chapter, but one bears repeating: God Loves Us! It is a love that is aggressive, whole-hearted and unmerited. When we begin to open our hearts to this amazing love, our inner life is transformed. Self-control is but one of the byproducts of this transformation process.

> "For the grace of God that brings salvation has appeared to all men. It teaches us to say 'No' to ungodliness and worldly passions, and to live self-controlled, upright and godly lives in this present age...."
> —*Titus 2:11,12*

Recommended Reading:

Manning, Brennan. *The Ragamuffin Gospel.* Sisters: Multnomah Publishers, 1990. This book has great insights into God's grace and unconditional love for us.

Wallis, Arthur. *God's Chosen Fast.* Ft. Washington: Christian Literature Crusade, 1974.

Bragg, Paul C. *The Miracle of Fasting.* Santa Barbara: Heath Science, 1981.

Fuhrman, M.D., Joel. *Fasting and Eating for Health.* St. Marin's Press, 1995.

Wheat and Perkins. *Love Life for Every Married Couple.* New York: Harper Collins, 1980.

Minirth, Frank. *Love Hunger: Recovery from Food Addiction.* Fawcett Books, May 1991.

The 12 Steps, A Way Out: A Spiritual Process for Healing Damaged Emotions. San Diego: Recovery Publications, 1995.

CHAPTER SIX
◆

Keeping in Touch

Recently, I saw a patient for follow-up discussion on weight control. At a previous appointment, Lisa (not her real name) said she had lost about 15 pounds by doing a Daniel-type diet, and she was thrilled with her progress. Though she still had a significant amount of weight to shed, she had made a good start on the road to better health.

However, on this latest visit she refused to let my medical assistant weigh her. Through tears she confessed to blowing the diet. This had been her pattern with diets: she would succeed in losing ten, 15 or even 30 pounds, but then seemed to sabotage any progress she made. She would begin overeating, feel guilty and ask herself, "What's the use of dieting?" After a few days or weeks of eating poorly, she would gain back the weight she had lost, or even more. She asked me what she could do to prevent this cycle from recurring.

I said there would definitely be a next time because she is human and can't do it perfectly. But then I asked her what kind of support she had for staying on her diet. Was there anyone she could talk to who would encourage her, listen without condemning and pray for her? She admitted she had no such person.

We talked about eating disorders and how people tend to use food as a substitute for lots of things that may have been missing in their lives – like parental love and acceptance, affirmation or attention. In her case, I suggested she start by finding one or two friends who could support and pray for her during this process. When she said she disliked asking for help, especially with this weight problem, I confronted her, "Lisa, you cannot do this alone."

> "God sets the lonely in families."
> —*Psalm 68:6a*

It Is Not Good To Be Alone

Life is more difficult alone. Whether we are dealing with a health issue, financial stress, death of a loved one or moving to a new city, life is harder when we face it alone. God Himself said so. After He made Adam and placed him in a beautiful garden with fresh fruits and vegetables readily available and delightful animals all around, even in this paradise on earth, God knew, *It is not good for the man to be alone* (Gen. 2:18). Medical science is now echoing this truth.

The Lancet, a prominent medical journal, affirmed the significance of patient support in publishing results of Dr. David Spiegel's study of 86 women with metastatic breast cancer. The patients were randomly divided into two groups. One received weekly support group therapy; the control group did not. Both groups continued to receive the same medical therapy. The purpose of the study was to see what effect a support group would have on the patients' *quality* of life – issues like pain control, depression and anxiety. Surprisingly, *quantity* of life was also effected – the treatment group, on average, lived twice as long as the control group. Having a supportive group (or family) made all the difference in outcome.[55]

Even more remarkable are two similar but separate studies involving over 20,000 participants and lasting from five to nine years. The participants were divided into groups based on social connectedness. The socially isolated group had a risk of death two to three times more than those who felt most connected to others.[56]

An article published in the journal *Science* under the title, "Social Relationships and Health," reviewed evidence from scientific studies such as the ones I've mentioned, and came up with this conclusion: *Social isolation is as significant to mortality rates as smoking, high blood pressure, high cholesterol, obesity, and lack of physical exercise. In fact, when age is adjusted for, social isolation is as great or greater a mortality risk than smoking.*[57] Science is merely confirming what God has said. It is not good to be alone!

There is mounting evidence that even the companionship of a pet can bring health benefits to those who are isolated. Pet therapy is being used increasingly in nursing homes, hospitals and for home-bound patients with excellent results. Of course, God's original answer to loneliness was not support groups or pet therapy, despite their proven benefits. Instead, God designed marriage and family to help meet our need for intimacy and closeness.

> "What is a Christian family?
> It is simply a unit of warm human love
> where God raises His imperfect sons.
> Truly we *are* called to give affection,
> pray with our children, attend church
> with them, discipline, and live before
> them an exemplary life, but
> it is God who will do the rest.
> In whatever ways we fail to do these
> simple things, it is God who will redeem."
> —*John & Paula Sandford*
> *in* Restoring the Christian Family

Studies comparing the health of married people and single people confirm the benefits of such relationships. Despite all the problems in marriages today, the studies consistently show that married people enjoy better health and greater longevity than their single counterparts.

Many studies also compare children raised in a traditional two-parent family and those raised by a single parent. The children from the two-parent family are healthier and less likely to drop out of school or exhibit violent behavior. This is not to put down single parents, who are struggling to give their children everything they need. It is to say that in an imperfect world, including when the nuclear family is absent or dysfunctional, kids suffer.

Even as pain in our physical body causes us to seek solutions, I believe God allows emotional pain and loneliness to point us to healthier options. Since God knows it's not good for us to be alone, He will provide for our needs. This might involve a support group, pet therapy or any number of social outlets. But again, God has designed His own peculiar solution to social isolation and loneliness – the "family of God."

The "Family of God"

Besides the nuclear family, God designed the church to be a type of family. The church can fill in gaps missing in our imperfect family situations. As part of the church, we all have one Father God and one Savior, who died for the sins of all people. In that commonality we find fellowship. Together we are the "bride of Christ," holy and pure because of what Christ has done on the cross. Yet we are also the "body of Christ," united under the headship of Jesus, yet diverse in function like the different parts of a body. We are the universal "catholic" church – open to all races, nationalities and socioeconomic classes.

Unfortunately, the church has struggled to follow God's design. She has, at times, been an embarrassing representation of Christ's body on earth. Over the centuries, the church has fostered exclusion and racism, and supported murderous crusades and inquisitions. Today, we continue to see prejudice and division and the tragic results of Christian leaders who abuse their authority or excuse immorality.

Though imperfect, the church still provides a haven of refuge for the lost to be rescued, the sick restored and the lonely embraced. The early church was a remarkable example of what the Christian community can be – free in sharing possessions, rich in fellowship and committed to spiritual training and worship. Ideally, the church provides everything a support group does and much more. It gives acceptance, encouragement, fellowship and a listening ear. More importantly, it teaches people how to know God. When functioning as designed, the family and church provide life-giving relationships that can overcome loneliness and enhance our overall physical and mental health.

The power of community

One obvious benefit of relationship is greater personal security. If someone is lost in the mountains, he has a greater chance of survival if he is not alone. Likewise, people in groups are less likely to be the target of criminal activity than those who are alone. In a recent *Focus on the Family* magazine article, Stu Weber describes the impact of friendship on one of the most traumatic experiences of his life. He says if it hadn't been for his new-found friend, Stevie McDonald, he's not sure if he would have made it through that first day of kindergarten.[58]

> "Two are better than one, because they have a good return for their work:
> If one falls down,
> his friend can help him up.
> But pity the man who falls
> and has no one to help him up!
> Also, if two lie down together,
> they will keep warm.
> But how can one keep warm alone?
> Though one may be overpowered,
> two can defend themselves.
> A cord of three strands
> is not quickly broken."
> —*Ecclessiastes 4:9-12*

The power of community demonstrates the power of synergy. Synergy is when the combined effect of the group is greater than the sum of its individual parts. Solomon illustrates this principle with the three-stranded rope. If the rope has only one strand, it can withstand a certain amount of tension – let's assume 50 pounds of tension. If the rope has two strands it can withstand not 50 + 50, but more than 100 pounds of tension. If three strands, it can withstand much more than 150 pounds of tension. The same principle is true when you use pulleys. If you have just one pulley, the effort you need to lift an object is the same as if there was no pulley. But as you add more pulleys, the effort decreases dramatically!

Synergy multiplies our strength and divides our effort. God designed the physical universe to work that way and synergy also works with people. "Many hands make light work" is something our family experiences when we work together to clean the house or do yard work. Yet the power of community is not just a mathematical phenomenon.

The third strand that is present in our marriage, our family, our friendships and in all our relationships – is Father God. He is the true source of power and strength in all relationships.

A couple of years ago, my wife and I became involved in a network marketing company. The general idea behind these companies is the power of geometric progression. This is how geometric progression works: I use the products the company markets and find my favorites. These I recommend to others. Some of these will sign up as distributors, use the products and recommend them to others. Some of these will sign up as distributors and so forth. If I sponsor four people, and each of these four people sponsors four more people, and each of these 16 people sponsors four more people, and each of these 64 people sponsor four people, and so forth... then I have a large organization. Each one is buying and using some of the product. When I have a large organization like that, I don't need to sell a lot individually. Instead of a few people selling a lot, there are a lot of people selling a little. And I have created residual income, just like someone who writes a book or records a song and continues to receive royalties years later.

"Operation Timothy" is based on the same idea. If I take a new friend through this discipleship program every two years, and they, in turn, begin to do the same thing, the number of people touched grows geometrically.

Jesus lived out this principle while on earth. He chose 12 apostles and entrusted them with His words and teachings. After Jesus left the earth, these 12 made other disciples. These new disciples, in turn, made other disciples who, in turn, made other disciples who made other disciples – until the known world had heard the gospel.

> "If two of you agree on earth
> about anything they ask, it will be done
> for them by my Father in heaven.
> For where two or three
> are gathered in my name,
> there am I in the midst of them."
> —*Matthew 18:19,20 (RSV)*

Bigger is not better

If two is better than one, then seven is better still, and 25 even better – and having the most is the best of all. Right? Wrong. A cord of 10 strands may be very difficult to break, but it also is too large for many practical jobs.

There are definite disadvantages to large groups, large cities, large businesses, large churches. One of the disadvantages is the difficulty in establishing relationships. There are a lot of faces, but no names. People get lost in the crowd, and when they don't make it to church, no one notices. The only way a large church can truly make a lasting impact on people is with small groups.

In the past few years, the growing Christian men's movement, called Promise Keepers, has received the most public attention from its large gatherings of men in sports stadiums. Our first PK event in Fresno's Bulldog Stadium drew close to 50,000 men – all worshipping our Lord, praying and listening to wonderful teaching. It was a goose-bump type of spiritual experience, and I will not be the same because of it. Yet as wonderful as it was, the power behind the PK movement is in the many small groups of men who gather every week to share their struggles, read their Bibles and pray for each other.

> "A Promise Keeper is committed to pursuing vital relationships with a few other men, understanding that he needs brothers to help him keep his promises."
> —*The second promise of a Promise Keeper*

During the summer of 1975, I was persuaded by Max Lucado (now a top Christian author) to join him and a couple other college friends to sell Bible Dictionaries door-to-door. We traveled to Nashville for a week of training and memorizing canned sales pitches, then split up in groups of two or three to designated areas. The work was hard – over

80 hours a week with only Sundays off. The weather was humid in Alabama where I was assigned. The people were friendly, but usually they weren't interested. I thought of quitting several times, but there were two things that kept me going.

One was my roommate, Don. We had never met before that summer. He was from the Northeast and I was from the West Coast. He was a Bible major and I was in science. We came from different denominational backgrounds. We really did not have many of the same interests, but we were placed together that summer and our common interest became to survive this difficult work experience. We got up early each morning and ate breakfast at a small downtown cafe in Jasper. We prayed together. We shared our fears and our dreams. I do not know where Don is now, but during that summer of 1975, he helped me to stick it out.

The second thing that kept me going was the weekly Sunday morning church services and meetings with my friends from college. I looked forward to those times of worship more than anything else. We sang praises with gusto, often with tears in our eyes, thankful to the Lord we had made it through another week, and thankful we had each other when we desperately missed our families and home-cooked meals (not necessarily in that order). After church we ate together, shared experiences from the previous week, laughed and generally supported each other. This was my first experience with an accountability group, and it was life-changing.

Jesus knew the power of community. He sent out 72 people to minister in the towns he was about to visit. They went out in pairs – two by two. Paul also knew. He did not go on his missionary journeys alone. He was accompanied by Barnabas, John Mark, Silas, Timothy or Luke. He had other close relationships with Titus and Epaphroditus. Paul needed others. Jesus needed others. We also need others.

Independence vs. Interdependence

Our country was born out of a Declaration of Independence from Great Britain. The Revolutionary War showed the tenacity of the American Minutemen and how the underdog settlers upset the more highly trained British Regulars. Ever since, our country has greatly valued rugged individualism. The pioneer spirit and "can do" attitude caused men and women to overcome the obstacles of wilderness living. It is demonstrated today in such things as space exploration and technological advances.

Independence is good. There are times when we need to break away from the past and be independent from certain relationships. For teenagers, gaining independence is a necessary step toward maturity.

Some people get stuck in the state of dependence. As children, we depended on our parents for everything. If children do not mature emotionally, they can continue in this state, thinking they are incapable of providing for their needs. They may become dependent on friends or the government for security and resources. The friends, the government or the parents then become co-dependent. They see their role as a caretaker, and though they may resent it at times, their actions and attitudes feed into this unhealthy arrangement.

In contrast is the state of interdependence. Here everyone contributes – and everyone receives. Everyone realizes he can't make it alone, and everyone realizes he has something significant to give.

> "Dependence is the paradigm of you – you take care of me. Independence is the paradigm of I – I am self-reliant. Interdependence is the paradigm of we – we can do it; we can combine our talents and abilities to create something greater together."
>
> —*Stephen Covey*

This was the state of the early church. Richard Foster describes it this way:

> *...the gifts of the Spirit were given by the [Holy] Spirit to the body in such a way that interdependence was insured. No one person possessed everything. Even the most mature needed the help of others. The most insignificant had something to contribute. No one could hear the whole counsel of God in isolation.*[59]

This is true of our physical bodies. Each part contributes, each is important, each has a different function. There is an amazing degree of interdependence. For the body to run smoothly it is designed with various feedback mechanisms. One such loop involves the thyroid gland and metabolism. In the lower part of the brain is the pituitary gland. This gland produces several hormones, one of which is called thyroid-stimulating hormone. Thyroid-stimulating hormone (or TSH) as its name implies, travels through the blood stream to the thyroid gland and stimulates it to produce thyroid hormone. This hormone goes throughout the body and affects our physiology – digestion, skin, temperature regulation and cardiac function. Thyroid hormone also goes back to the brain, instructing it to slow down the production of TSH which, in turn, slows down the production of thyroid hormone.

This is a simplified explanation – but it could be likened to the heating system in our homes. The pituitary gland would be the thermostat, TSH the electricity and the thyroid hormone the heat. When the heat reaches a certain point, the thermostat cuts off the electricity until the temperature drops far enough. Then the thermostat switches on the electricity again.

Sometimes when the TSH instructs the thyroid gland to produce more hormone, the thyroid is incapable of responding, either because of prior infection, inflammation or surgical removal. Without the production of thyroid hormone, the feedback mechanism is not engaged, and the pituitary gland continues to produce more and more TSH.

In community, we need feedback mechanisms as well. We need encouragement, love, physical contact and appreciation. We also need counsel, criticism, instruction and confrontation. If we are in the loop, engaged and involved with people who care, this can happen. If we are outside the loop, we miss out. We are like the unresponsive thyroid gland – oblivious to the needs of the body. Or we can be like the shouting pituitary gland – asking for help, but getting no response.

The vulnerability of sharing our lives, of being learners, exposing who we really are and our innermost dreams, can be a frightful place. Yet that vulnerability keeps us in the loop, and when we are connected, it is amazing what can happen. The story of how my sabbatical was birthed in Chapter 1 is an example. It began with already having community with my wife and brother-in-law and their prayers. It was then safe to share my dreams and receive feedback and encouragement. To get from dream to reality, I enlisted a group of about ten people to pray, updating them frequently about the status of my journey. Through community a dream became reality!

> "We all must hang together, or assuredly we shall all hang separately."
> —*Benjamin Franklin*

This book is about our physical body being the temple of God's Spirit. When we, as individuals, join together to worship Jesus and do His work, we are each an important part of something wonderful – God's body on earth. We are God's hands to do His will and work, to touch each other and those who don't know Him. One facet of this kind of community involves physical touch.

The Necessity of Physical Touch

It is a step of faith to leave the walls of isolation and experience physical contact with people. For not only are we exposing ourselves to positive touch such as a handshake or hug, we also expose ourselves to potential hurt and rejection. If we look closely, even the friendly, positive touch of a handshake can be a dangerous action. For on our hands are millions of tiny germs that can be transferred to one another and cause symptoms as mild as a cold or as deadly as meningitis.

To help His people guard against disease, God instituted regulations that form the basis for what are now commonly accepted public health principles. His laws in Leviticus and Deuteronomy are the first in recorded human history to deal with the spread of infectious diseases through patient isolation, keeping human elimination away from the camp where it could not contaminate water or food, and requiring the washing of hands. There were even regulations involving infectious discharges touching clothes or furniture, and how these articles might transmit the disease. This may seem rather basic until we remember the germ theory of disease was not discovered until the 1800s!

Despite the danger that may be present when we touch another human being, the danger of not touching is even greater. In the nineteenth century, infants had less than a 50 percent chance of surviving their first year of life. As late as the 1920s, the death rate in some U.S. foundling institutions was even higher – sometimes approaching 100 percent! What was the cause of this dismal statistic? They called it marasmus or wasting disease. Today, we call it failure to thrive. But what was behind this unnecessary tragedy?

In 1894, Emmett Holt Sr., a professor of pediatrics at Columbia University wrote a booklet entitled, *The Care and Feeding of Children*. Over the next 25 to 30 years, it became the standard authority for infant and child care. In the booklet, Dr. Holt warned that picking up babies when they cry could spoil them. He encouraged a distant, sterile relationship.

The high death rates in the orphanages were due, primarily, to following the guidelines in this booklet. Another pediatrician, Henry Chapin, noted the high death rate and the lack of physical touch between the babies and the adult workers. He brought in women to hold, rock and stroke them – and the mortality rate dropped dramatically!

> "People were bringing little children to Jesus to have Him touch them...."
> —Mark 10:13

Our bodies must perceive through touch. For example, a diabetic who develops neuropathy may lose touch perception in his feet and can be in danger from something as innocuous as a small pebble in his shoe. The pebble can cause a sore which, if undetected, might eventually lead to ulceration, infection and sometimes amputation. Leprosy is similar. It also affects the body's nerve cells. The leper may not feel pain when he grabs a hot iron skillet, for example, and without natural pain perception, severe damage can result.

But even more important than pain perception, the body needs human touch. Alan McGinnis writes about our skin: *As a sensory system it is the most important organ of the body. A human being can function blind and deaf and completely lacking the senses of smell and taste, but it is impossible to survive at all without the function performed by the skin.*[60]

Whether we are incurable romantics or bottom-line statisticians, everyone of us needs human touch. The two or three handshakes we may get during the day are not enough. Someone has suggested that for optimum emotional health we need eight hugs a day.

Recently, I took my daughter Sarah, and three of her friends, to the Six Flags amusement park in Valencia, California. By the end of the day I was tired and sat down on a bench to rest. As I was resting, I watched Daffy Duck interacting with the children and adults who were walking by. Daffy never said a word. He just waved, touched shoulders, and gave hugs to the hundreds of people he encountered. I thought that would be a fun job – giving hundreds of hugs all day long.

Parents brought children to Jesus in New Testament times so He could touch them. This was not necessarily for miraculous, physical healing. Yet something miraculous happened. A blessing was transmitted from Jesus to the children. In Old Testament times, the father transmitted his blessings to his children through touch. When we touch someone we, too, can impart a gift of blessing.

The Laying On of Hands

The Bible describes many instances in which the laying on of hands imparts a spiritual gift, a blessing, a physical healing or an anointing for ministry. In Acts 13, the church at Antioch placed hands on Paul and Barnabas as they prayed before their first missionary journey. In Acts 8, Peter and John touched believers so they could receive the Holy Spirit.

Many of the physical healings recorded in the Gospels involved touch. It is interesting to note that those healings which did *not* include physical touch, most often were when Jesus was in the midst of a watching crowd or dealing with demon possession. When a healing was a one-on-one encounter between Jesus and an afflicted person, Jesus invariably used physical touch.

Healings also resulted when people reached out and touched Jesus. The woman with abnormal vaginal bleeding did this. She was instantly healed. Similarly, in Gennesaret, a group of sick people found healing when they reached out and touched Jesus' cloak.

Later, Peter and Paul fulfill the Lord's promise that greater miracles would follow. In Acts 5, people in Jerusalem brought the sick and placed them on mats in the street, hoping that Peter's shadow would touch them as he walked past. It is implied that these people were healed. In Acts 19, while Paul was in Ephesus, *God did extraordinary miracles through Paul. Handkerchiefs and aprons that had touched him were taken to the sick, and their illnesses were cured and the evil spirits left them.* Even as a cloth containing infectious material might cause sickness, a cloth touched by the power of God can bring healing.

It is clear that touch was a significant part of the healing miracles of Jesus. I believe today, touch continues to be part of our physical and emotional healing and a preventive health principle we can incorporate into our lives.

Massage

One way to receive healing touch is through therapeutic massage. As noted in Chapter 2, we often live with high levels of daily stress. At the same time, our bodies are crying out for physical contact. The "hands-on" approach of a regular massage can address both of these areas.

Massage has several benefits for the body:

- it can increase the circulation of the blood and the lymph
- it can help relax tightened muscles
- it can help stimulate weak, flaccid muscles
- it can help bring relaxation or stimulation to the nervous system
- it can aid in recovery of strains or sprains
- it can help relieve stress and tension
- it can be a natural solution to common ailments like headaches, insomnia or anxiety.

When was the last time you received a massage? A dentist friend of mine gets a massage every week. He spends the time in his office stooping over screaming, squirming children several hours a day. By the end of the week, his back and neck muscles are tight and uncomfortable. He has learned that he needs regular body work in order to take care of himself and continue serving effectively.

Growing up, my brother and I would often give each other back rubs at night (when we weren't trying to scare each other in the dark). It was amazing how effective they were in promoting relaxation and improved sleep. As an adult, I was reintroduced to massage through my brother-in-law, a massage therapist in St. Paul, Minnesota. In addition to the physical touch of his hands, he also incorporates inner healing prayer – touching the soul as well. The combined effect on the mind and body is wonderfully therapeutic.

In looking for a personal massage therapist, ask your physician, your friends or even your church leaders for their recommendations. Trust is a big issue in this field and it helps to have a referral from someone you respect. If you cannot afford this on a regular basis, do it when you can, and supplement the interim times with massages from your spouse, your family or a friend.

Intimate Touch

Sensual touch between a man and a woman is one of the most pleasurable gifts God has given to married couples. God designed the woman's breasts and the genitals of both sexes to be very sensitive to loving touch.

Just as touch is a key to pleasurable sexual function, touch is also a key to healing sexual dysfunction. When a couple is struggling with a sexual problem in their relationship, it can bring great stress into other aspects of their lives. The most common sexual dysfunction for men is impotence, and for women, the inability to achieve an orgasm. Though there are numerous etiologies for these dysfunctions, the most likely one is that the husband and wife are (as McGinnis describes it), "out of touch" with one another.

The prescription involves learning to touch each other. Here is how McGinnis describes it:

> *Choose a time when you can lock the bedroom door and will not be disturbed, but not late at night when you are both exhausted. Now lie together naked on the bed. For the first 20 minutes, one is the giver, one is the receiver. As receiver your sole task is to lie quietly and let your partner caress you. Do not caress back, do not look around, and do not talk, except to tell your partner what feels good, where you'd like to be touched more lightly, where more firmly. As your partner lightly rubs lotion into your body, become aware of the variety of sensations which your skin is receiving. This is not foreplay, and we advise that for a few sessions the couple avoid touching the breasts and genitals in the exercise.*
>
> *And no sex afterward! Why? Because without thinking about what is coming afterward or worrying about performance later, you can give 100% of your concentration to what you are feeling through your skin. After 20 minutes of such pleasuring, switch roles.*[61]

If sexual dysfunctions are not improving after two or three weeks of this kind of touch therapy, then other causes need to be explored. I would recommend a visit to your family physician or health care provider to discuss this and see if further testing is needed.

Recommendations

1. **Explore your family of origin – your first community.** Rejoice and celebrate the good. Seek healing from any dysfunctions. Learning about what is and isn't normal might be the first step. This can happen through reading books or participating in a 12-step

group. Counseling might be beneficial. If dysfunctions are identified, choices can be made to begin the process of forgiveness and releasing hurts.

Next evaluate your present family. Is it functioning normally? Consider ways you can better support each other. Praying for each other is a great beginning. Learning to communicate is a big key. Having family traditions, special family vacations or outings, weekly family nights, regular dates with your spouse and each child – all can add to family cohesiveness that can help overcome the most difficult times.

2. **Embrace your church community.** We all need a church where there is open and honest concern for each other – where if one suffers, all suffer with them; if one rejoices, all rejoice with them. Look at the example of the New Testament church to find new ways of loving, supporting and encouraging each other.

3. **Invest in friendship.** We all need one to three close friends. If you are married, your spouse can certainly be a great friend and confidant. But you really need same-sex friends with whom you feel comfortable, who can listen, support and pray for you.

For men, with the growing number of Promise Keeper groups being started, this might be a place to start. If your church has no men's ministry, talk to your pastor and some other men about starting some small groups. For women, it is usually easy to find a women's Bible study group at church. If this is not what you need, consider starting a support group, a prayer group or a worship group.

Tips for building friendships

- The first step in looking for friends is to **pray**. Don't be blinded by preconceptions of what you think you need in a friend. The Lord may have other plans for you.

- **Be patient.** It takes time to get to know someone. It takes time to break through the superficial stuff and open up. It took me several years to develop relationships (after moving to Fresno) that have progressed into close friendships.

- You can't be close with everyone. Most people do well to **limit close friendships** to one to three people.

- **Make a list of potential friends.**

- **Take the initiative.** It might be just to go out for breakfast or lunch. It might be to share in a common interest like golf, walking or shopping.

- **Develop regular contact.** This is crucial. This is one reason it is so difficult to maintain relationships over long distances. We need to have regular contact. Usually this means face to face. However, I have friendships in which most of our contact is by phone once or twice a month to share needs and then pray together.

- **Practice relational skills.** One of the best books I've read on this subject is *The Friendship Factor* by Alan Loy McGinnis. He teaches how to deepen relationships through cultivating intimacy and transparency, making your relationships a top priority, learning the gestures of love and creating space in your relationships.

(Adapted from an article by Stu Weber. See endnote 58.)

4. **Consider getting a Spiritual Director.** The idea of a Spiritual Director is largely unknown and unpracticed outside the Catholic church. Richard Foster writes this about it:

What is the purpose of a spiritual director? The seventeenth-century Benedictine mystic, Dom Augustine Baker, wrote, 'In a word, he is only God's usher, and must lead souls in God's way and not his own.' His direction is simply and clearly to lead us to our real Director.[62]

Basically, the spiritual director is an advisor, a brother or sister we can learn from, who has shown maturity in their travels with the Master and who has some gifts in discernment.

5. **Give and receive healthy touch on a regular basis.** If you are married and have children, one idea is to give each other massages on a regular basis. Another is to remember to touch your family members – give lots of hugs; rock your kids or your spouse; touch them as you pass in the kitchen or hall. Consider getting regular therapeutic massage.

Spiritual Connection – Communing with the Head of the Body

God Himself teaches us something about community in His triune nature. He is the one true God, and He is also God the Father, God the Son and God the Holy Spirit. God in three persons. He also reached out and touched mankind by sending Jesus in human form to planet earth. God in human flesh. God reached out and touched man, and man was able to reach out and touch Him back.

And because of God, we now, having God's Spirit inside our bodies, can find communion with God, community with each other and the power of touch that can heal, comfort and bless.

Recommended Reading:

Welch, Reuben. *We Really Do Need Each Other.* Grand Rapids: Zondervan, 1973.

McGinnis, Alan Loy. *The Friendship Factor.* Minneapolis: Augsberg Publishing House, 1979.

CHAPTER SEVEN

Learn to Celebrate

Winter solstice. Traditionally, a time of celebration both in ancient and medieval times. In 1977, it was a time of celebration for Kathryn Morris, Ron Kleyn (me), and our families as Katie and I joined our hearts and lives together in holy matrimony. And it was not your usual winter wedding.

First, it was outdoors in the backyard of Katie's parents in Baytown, Texas. Though we were blessed with sunshine, I still remember the chill bumps from both nervousness and the brisk air. Second, the occasion was in the middle of the week to allow relatives from California to get back in time for Christmas. Third, we sang to each other. Something we were never asked to do again (not because of Katie's voice, either).

Still things were going well – until near the end of the ceremony when it was time for exchanging rings. I was supposed to have her ring in my pocket, but I had forgotten. It was still in a suitcase inside my in-laws' home. I ran to get it while the guests warmed by chuckling a bit. It was not the only thing I forgot that week. After the first night of our honeymoon, we left Galveston Island to spend a few days at Lake Travis, but left behind, in the Flagship Hotel room, my favorite casual shoes. Katie and I have often laughed together, reminded of the Norman Rockwell painting of hotel housekeeping personnel working in a honeymoon suite holding up a left-behind shoe.

Laughter is Good Medicine

There is something about laughter that soothes the soul, the spirit and the body. Embracing our human condition with all of its frailties and imperfections (including forgetfulness), requires both grace and the ability to laugh at ourselves. The alternative is not only a bland existence, but an unhealthy one.

Proverbs 17:22 says, *A cheerful heart is good medicine, but a crushed spirit dries up the bones*. While most of us know this intuitively, only during the past three decades has medical science tried to figure out how and why laughter and celebration benefit our health.

Ironically, the first significant research on the subject was not by a medical researcher, but by Norman Cousins, former editor of the *Saturday Review*. Cousins suffered from a severe type of arthritis called *ankylosing spondylitis*. When anti-inflammatory medications failed to give him relief, Cousins began to look at alternative measures. He was particularly interested in how emotions affect one's physical health. Cousins theorized that if negative emotions like fear, shame and anxiety could adversely affect the body, then conversely, positive emotions would have a positive effect on our health.

> "A light heart lives long."
> —*Shakespeare*

He began to watch old Marx Brothers' movies, past episodes of "Candid Camera," and children's cartoons. The daily dose of humor had a dramatic effect on his arthritic condition, and Cousins wrote a book about his experiences.[63] He spent the rest of his life searching for a scientific explanation of his hypothesis.

The positive effect of laughter on the immune system was later affirmed in research by Lee Berk at Loma Linda University in California. Berk conducted experiments measuring the immune system's response to outside stimuli. One group was shown a video of a stand-up comic while the second group was separated in a quiet room. Both had IVs and blood samples were taken every ten minutes. The control group showed no physiological changes. The group watching the comedian showed significant increases in various measures of immune function. Berk concluded that laughter stimulates the immune system in a positive way. Just as stress causes the release and increase of adrenalin into the blood, laughter lowers it![64]

Stanford University professor William Fry discovered in his research on laughter that 100 laughs is the aerobic equivalent to ten minutes on a rowing machine. Row, row, rowing your boat can be replaced with merrily, merrily, merrily laughing your waistline away![65]

As information about the health benefits of humor has spread worldwide, the inevitable has happened: laughing clubs are springing up. In India, club members meet in a park every morning to laugh together. They do not tell jokes, though that's how it started. Their routine begins with some warm-up exercises with everyone shouting, "Ho-ho, ha-ha," in unison. Then they raise their arms above their heads and laugh (out loud, then silently) for a few minutes. Then they are off to their daily duties.[66]

> "He who laughs, lasts."
> —*Anonymous*

I love to laugh

In the Disney classic *Mary Poppins*, there's a scene in which Bert takes Mary and the children to visit Uncle Albert (played by the late Ed Wynn). Uncle Albert tries to greet them, but he just can't sit still long enough. Every time he laughs (which is often), he becomes weightless and starts floating up to the room's high vaulted ceiling. Laughter does that. It helps us soar above the serious and the mundane. It melts tensions and temporarily lifts us above our troubles. Of course, it's possible to get too much of a good thing. In George MacDonald's *The Light Princess*, a daughter is cursed with weightlessness both in body and in spirit. Not only can she float away if her attendants aren't careful, but she is constantly lighthearted in word and thought. She cannot be serious. Therefore she has no substance, no depth.

Obviously we need a balance. I tend to live on the sober side of life. Fortunately, God has placed in my life special people who are fun-loving, spontaneous and silly. My college roommate Mike, a consummate practical joker, was one. My wife Katie is another. She is a laugher *extraordinaire*. Her humor balances my cold and calculating side. And it's contagious!

This is serious

After my first semester at college, I was back home in California for Christmas vacation. I was tired and listless, so I asked my physician-father to check me over. After a thorough exam, and blood tests that came back normal, my wise father gave me his diagnosis: I was just too serious for my own good.

I had spent the past four years of high school pushing myself to be an honor student, and I was continuing that pattern in college. I was conscientious. I was responsible. I was reflective. All very noble qualities. Yet I had a serious problem. I needed to lighten up.

As with most periods of history, my time growing up (largely the 1960s and 1970s), left me with a lot to be serious about: the Vietnam war, the drug culture, racial tensions, assassinations of key leaders and the resignation of a president. In church, I was confronted with the seriousness of sin, the fear of hell and the obligation to reach the lost. There were questionings of authority and seekings for truth. Most of these problems are still with us today. All of them are serious and deserve thoughtful examination. But we tend to be overwhelmed with the serious side of life, and forget that God also is the author of laughter and joy.

Richard Foster, writing in *Celebration of Discipline* said,

Far and away the most important benefit of celebration is that it saves us from taking ourselves too seriously. That is a desperately needed grace for all those who are earnest about the spiritual disciplines. It is an occupational hazard of devout folk to become stuffy bores. That should not be. Of all people we should be the most free, alive, interesting. Celebration adds a note of gaiety, festivity, and hilarity to our lives. After all, Jesus rejoiced so fully in life that He was accused of being a wine-bib-

ber and a glutton. Many of us lead such sour lives that we couldn't possibly be accused of such things.[67]

Today has its own harsh realities. Pick up any newspaper or watch the evening news to find out the latest government scandal, natural disaster or depressing figures about crime or drugs or teenage pregnancy. We are inundated with the realities of sin in this world, a world gone amuck as people forget God and pursue their own lusts. It is enough to sober the most light-hearted among us. But with all these bad things happening, it is all the more reason for us to be bearers of good news. Our God is the author of the good news.

God Loves a Celebration

Celebration is part of God's plan for us, and He is our supreme example. Job 38:7 describes how *the angels shouted for joy* as they witnessed the creation. In Zephaniah 3:17 the prophet records how God Himself delights in His children and rejoices over us with singing. In Jesus' parable of the prodigal son, He reveals how God yearns for our communion and celebrates our returning to Him.

In the Old Testament, the Lord instituted feasts and festivals to require His overly serious people to set aside time to celebrate and remember their roots. These included the Feast of Unleavened Bread, the Feast of Harvest and the Feast of Ingathering (see Exodus 23:14-16) and various New Moon festivals. He also commanded them to set aside special times for celebrating the Passover and the Feast of Tabernacles. These weren't one-day holidays like we have in our culture. The celebration went on for days, sometimes weeks. When Solomon dedicated the temple, the whole nation of Israel celebrated for two weeks. In 1 Kings 8:66 it says that when the feasting ended, the people *blessed the king and then went home, joyful and glad in heart for all the good things the Lord had done for His servant David and His people Israel.*

Each festival was deeply meaningful to the Jewish people, either as a reminder of God's deliverance in the past or a reminder of God's provision in the present. It was a time of celebration. Usually this involved gathering together as a people, abstaining from work and enjoying a meal together. More spontaneous celebrations occurred after God gave them victory over their enemies (1 Samuel 18:6), when they were delivered from captivity and when the temple was built (and rebuilt). In addition, every week they were to keep the Sabbath day, every seven years an entire year was a Sabbath year (or sabbatical) and every 50 years, a Year of Jubilee.

Today, in America, we also celebrate some significant holidays: the gaining of our independence from England; the honoring of our war veterans and those who gave their lives for this country; a feast of Thanksgiving for God's provision; Jesus' birth; and Jesus' resurrection. We can learn how to make these holidays special, to transform them from a three-day weekend to a celebration that incorporates the meaning behind the festival.

Singing, music and dancing were often part of the Jewish festivals. Music, like laughter, can be a powerful key to remove inhibitions and defenses, and be touched by the living God.* A few years ago, our church sent a group of our youth to Mexico for a service project at a small church near Tijuana. One night after the service, the Holy Spirit filled the little church and spontaneously everyone in attendance

---

* The enemy knows this well and uses music for promoting drugs, sex and violence. Just as praise and affirmation transmitted through music can positively affect world view, so also can our minds be negatively affected by repeated exposure to gross and destructive lyrics.

began to dance before the Lord. No one was wondering what other people were thinking. A special gift of celebration had descended on this group and everyone was blessed as they freely praised God!

Become childlike

Children are the experts on celebration. They laugh, they giggle, they play, they sing and dance without inhibition. So when Jesus said, *Anyone who will not receive the kingdom of God like a little child will never enter it* (Mark 10:15), He was challenging us to receive Him and rejoice in Him with childlike simplicity. One of the ways children teach us how to enter the kingdom is in their ability to receive. They accept gifts much more freely than adults.

> "Let the little children come to me,
> and do not hinder them,
> for the kingdom of heaven
> belongs to such as these."
> —*Jesus in Matthew 19:14*

Consider this restaurant scene. Two friends are having an enjoyable conversation and meal. Then the check comes, and with it, an awkward silence. One says politely, "Here, let me take that."

Then the other jumps in, "Oh no way, I can't let you do that."

"Mighty generous of you," he replies, "but you fed me last week in your home."

"Yes, and I'm going to feed you today too, whether you like it or not."

I wonder – do we do the same thing with God? Is He

sometimes trying to give blessings beyond measure, but instead of accepting them with joy, we self-sufficiently and politely say, "I can take care of that myself"?

A more childlike (and Christ-like) example is that of a colleague of my father who once accompanied us to a college-produced musical. As we were walking up to the auditorium my father said to him, "Now I want you to realize your ticket is already paid for, and this is our treat." I braced myself for the usual stand-off, but surprisingly (and refreshingly), he said, "Oh, that's very nice of you. Thank you very much." This man's ability to accept this gift with sincere gratitude deeply impressed me. It hit me later that it was the childlikeness of this man's acceptance that was so unique. Childlike acceptance, without adult games, is how Jesus calls us to receive Him.

Children are masters at play. They can pretend, they can dream, they can utilize their imaginations. Getting in touch with our inner child is not some weird, New Age thing. It is part of coming to Jesus as a child. And it can be a great gift for us in learning how to celebrate.

A book by Tom Mullen hits the heart of this issue in a story about James Russell Lowell:

> *When passing a building in the outskirts of Boston, [Lowell] noticed an identifying inscription: 'Home for Incurable Children'. To a friend he remarked, 'They'll get me in there some day.' That's a worthwhile wish for ourselves, too. If we would enter the Kingdom, that is exactly what we'll need to be – **incurable** children.*[68]

But I feel like crying

One of my favorite characters in children's literature is Puddleglum in C.S. Lewis' *The Silver Chair*. Puddleglum is so serious and negative about everything, that it's actually funny to read about him. As he and his two companions are traveling through the magical kingdom of Narnia, Puddleglum is forever reminding them of the disasters that may overtake them. Sometimes when Katie or I get stuck in a "serious mud hole" of gloom, the other impersonates Puddleglum and recites a laundry list of absurdly negative possibilities to our predicament. It often works to bring light and humor to the situation.

The Bible makes it clear that we are to rejoice in Him even when things *aren't* going so well. This is a response of faith, a recognition that God is in control of all things, even our present circumstances. Habbakuk 3:17-18 says,

> *Though the fig tree does not bud and there are no grapes on the vines, though the olive crop fails and the fields produce no food, though there are no sheep in the pen and no cattle in the stalls, yet I will rejoice in the Lord, I will be joyful in God my Savior.*

And Jesus said in Luke 6:22-23:

> *Blessed are you when men hate you, when they exclude you and insult you and reject your name as evil, because of the Son of Man. Rejoice in that day and leap for joy, because great is your reward in heaven. For that is how their fathers treated the prophets.*

Peter and his fellow apostles certainly put this into practice. After being flogged for speaking out about Jesus, they *left the Sanhedrin, rejoicing because they had been counted worthy of suffering disgrace for the Name* (Acts 5:41).

Jesus taught that we can rejoice, not only in our circumstances, but despite them. This is not an invitation to deny our feelings. The reason we can rejoice in the midst of pain or suffering is that joy is deeper than circumstances.

Circumstances are temporary and sometimes out of our control. The joy of the Lord is eternal and based on God's unchanging character – His mercy, love and grace.

Remember the connection we made with fear and anxiety? Many of our stresses are birthed from fear. We have many cares in this world, but God is asking us to *be careful for nothing* (Phil. 4:6 KJV). Foster writes,

> *When we trust God we are free to rely entirely upon Him to get what we need: "By prayer and supplication with thanksgiving let your requests be made known unto God." Prayer is the means by which we move the arm of God. Hence we can live in a spirit of carefree celebration.*[69]

> "Consider it pure joy, my brothers, whenever you face trials of many kinds."
> —James 1:2

This is the reason the Bible commands us to rejoice. It is a decision. Like the chorus says: "I will rejoice, for I've made my choice to rejoice in the Lord." And it is not merely rejoicing for rejoicing's sake. The object of our joy is the Lord. We rejoice in the Lord despite our external circumstances, despite our internal fears. He is God. We can trust in Him, and rejoice because of His faithfulness and our connection with Him. *Be joyful always; pray continually; give thanks in all circumstances, for this is God's will for you in Christ Jesus* (1 Thess. 5:16-18).

Express Your Feelings

Life is obviously full of emotions other than laughter, joy and celebration. God is not asking us to put up a false front when we experience one of life's tragedies or disappointments. The Bible's wisest king (Solomon) wrote, *There is... a time to weep and a time to laugh, a time to mourn and a time to dance* (Eccl. 3:4). In Proverbs 14 he wrote, *Each heart knows its own bitterness, and no one else can share its joy.*

Scripture is full of references of how grief can turn to joy (John 16:20); how joy can turn to gloom (Jas. 4:9); how weeping can turn to rejoicing (Ps. 30:5); and how jubilation can be taken away (Hos. 9:1).

Life reflects this dichotomy from beginning to end. Labor and childbirth can be extremely painful. Yet the mother forgets the pain *because of her joy that a child is born into the world* (John 16:21). Death may be prefaced by much suffering through sickness or pain. Family and friends also suffer because of separation from the one they love. Yet, for the believer, death is a new beginning of eternal bliss.

Who stole our joy?

Many people believe Christianity and humor are oxymorons. Because Christians talk about sin, hell and self-control, there is the tendency to see ourselves as puckered, stern-faced disciples of seriousness. Perhaps we can cast some of the blame toward our Puritan forefathers. In their pursuit of living pure lives for God, perhaps they overemphasized the disciplines and devotion, and under emphasized the freedom and joy we have in Christ.

Perhaps the Puritan concern was that the people of God would cross over from humor to folly. Proverbs 15:21 says, *Folly delights a man who lacks judgment, but a man of understanding keeps a straight course.* Certainly not all humor is good. Ethnic jokes can be cruel. Practical jokes can become mean-spirited. And television abounds with examples of humor that are debasing, sacrilegious or overtly sexual. We sometimes use sarcastic humor as veiled criticism in situations that we need to confront openly and honestly.

Again, we see how a healthy habit, given to us by God, can be twisted and used by Satan for evil purposes. Just as rest can become laziness; self-control can become asceticism; and dietary guidelines can become legalism; so, humor that is meant to be a tool to lighten our hearts, can turn into a weapon that cuts and stings.

I like the *Twelve Affirmations of Positive Humor* that Christian Hagaseth III, M.D., from the American Association of Therapeutic Humor has put together. Here's his list:

1) *I am determined to use my humor for positive, uplifting, healing, and loving purposes.*

2) *I will take myself lightly while I take my work in life seriously.*

3) *I will not seek to be offended by others attempts at humor. When in doubt, I will see others as meaning well.*

4) *I will express humor physically, using my whole face and (when so moved) my entire body.*

5) *I refuse to use my humor to camouflage hostility or prejudice.*

6) *I understand that the gift of laughter is a treasured gift, so I will laugh generously at others attempts to be humorous.*

7) *All teasing and ethnic humor will be by mutual consent and will go both ways or I will not engage in such humor.*

8) I will respect the forbidden topics of my listeners. I will avoid giving offense with my humor.

9) If I offend another by my use of humor, I will make amends.

10) I will be eternally vigilant for the jokes and absurdities of the universe, and I will share my observations with my companions in life.

11) In the midst of adversity, I will continue to use humor to cope, to survive, to heal, to grow, and to pass on loving kindness.

12) On the day of my death I will look back and know that I laughed lovingly, fully and well.[70]

One of the most significant benefits of humor is the ability to take ourselves and the things we cherish a little less seriously. Start collecting jokes and stories about your particular profession. One antidote for the seriousness of my work is to tell doctor jokes. Here are some examples I've collected:

- *I have a great doctor. He gave a guy six months to live. The guy couldn't pay his bill so he gave him another six months.*

- *He had to see his doctor in the morning for a blood test, so he stayed up all night studying for it.*

- *A patient confessed to her physician that she had first consulted her pastor and a faith healer regarding her health.*
    "And what foolish advice did they give you?" asked the doctor.
    "They both told me to see you."[71]

Ode to Joy

We are not talking about happiness. The pursuit of happiness, according to the Declaration of Independence, is one of our inalienable rights along with life and liberty. Yet attaining happiness seems to be dependent on externals: circumstances, living conditions, social structure, material possessions.

The Biblical alternative is joy. Joy is deeper. Joy is not dependent on circumstances. Joy is a state of being. Joy is a fruit of the Spirit. Joy is totally connected with the spiritual realm. Even though joy is independent of circumstances, there are actions we can take and attitudes of the heart that naturally lead to joy. This is not a cookbook recipe for producing joy, but rather a list of biblical insights and directions that will make it more likely for us to experience it.

What naturally leads to joy:

1. Being in God's presence – *You have made known to me the path of life; you will fill me with joy in your presence, with eternal pleasures at your right hand* (Psalm 16:11). The natural result of being in God's presence is greater joy. The church worldwide is experiencing greater freedom in worship. The raising of hands toward God and speaking out in corporate verbal praise – styles of worship only seen in charismatic churches a few years ago – are being practiced in many denominations today. As we freely worship God, we begin to see life from a heavenly perspective. Earthly cares fade away as we experience the joy of being with our Father God.

2. Experiencing God's deliverance – *But let all who take refuge in You be glad; let them ever sing for joy. Spread Your protection over them, that those who love your name* *may rejoice in You* (Psalm 5:11). Our first experience of God's deliverance is the moment He saves us from the consequences of our sin. Sin separates us from God. When we repent, confessing our sins and asking Him to take control, rejoicing breaks out in heaven (Luke 15:7) and in our own hearts as well. The "secret" in Hannah Whitall Smith's classic work, *The Christian's Secret of a Happy Life*, is that surrendering to Christ in obedience brings joy.

3. Applying the Word of God – *Your words are what sustain me; they are food to my hungry soul. They bring joy to my sorrowing heart and delight me. How proud I am to bear Your name, Lord* (Jer. 15:16 Amplified). God's Word nourishes our soul and helps us plant firm roots. In the Parable of the Sower, some seed fell on rocky soil and sprang up quickly. But these plants didn't last long because the soil was shallow and they had no roots (Matt. 13). We may begin with joy, receiving God's seed; but we must also develop roots by continued nourishment and spiritual food.

4. Being in fellowship – *We proclaim to you what we have seen and heard, so that you also may have fellowship with us. And our fellowship is with the Father and with his Son, Jesus Christ. We write this to make our joy complete* (1 John 1:3-4). Joy is not dependent on fellowship with one another but it sure helps. Laughing together is more fun than laughing alone. Being in community makes us vulnerable to greater pain, yet also allows us to experience greater joy (see Chapter 6).

> "Be joyful always... for this is God's will for you in Christ Jesus."
> —*1 Thessalonians 5:16-18*

5. Practicing generosity – There is a strong connection between giving and being lighthearted. When we are carefree, we are free to hold onto our possessions lightly and pass them on to others who need them more. The phrase Paul uses in 2 Corinthians 9:7, *God loves a cheerful giver*, could also be rendered, *God loves a hilarious giver*. It is wholehearted giving and it can create joy.

In Charles Dickens' *A Christmas Carol*, Scrooge was not only miserly, he was miserable. His life was devoid of joy and laughter. All was seriousness, work and greed. After his encounters with the three ghosts, he became generous and his life had joy. This principle is not limited to our finances. In *The Clown of God*, a juggler joins a monastery in an attempt to give his life to God. He discovers that what God wants is his talent. Using our talents for God is an act of generosity that can truly bring joy.

Joy and strength

I see many people in my office complaining of fatigue and lack of energy. A physical exam and blood tests almost always come back normal. So what is the problem? I believe it is often a lack of joy. Nehemiah 8:10 says, *the joy of the Lord is your strength*. Life without joy is dull and burdensome, no matter what its circumstances. For us to sustain any activity or project in life, joy must be present. Richard Foster says this is true of the Spiritual Disciplines, and I believe it applies to the Physical Disciplines or Health Habits outlined in this book: *Without a joyful spirit of festivity, these disciplines become dull, death-breathing tools in the hands of modern Pharisees. Every discipline should be characterized by carefree gaiety and a sense of thanksgiving.*[72]

When we look at the Christian church in America today, what do we see? Is it vibrant and healthy? Is it full of energy? Is it a strong witness to those around? Or is it tired and weak? Does it seem powerless and anemic? If the *joy of the Lord* brings strength, we need that joy individually as well as corporately. I can think of at least a couple of reasons.

The first is obvious. The church needs an infusion of joy. These are troubled times. God is the source of relief, release and unrestricted hilarity.

The second is probably the more important. Joy and laughter break down defenses. They open up our hearts and spirits. They put us in a vulnerable place where God can do a deeper work – where He can give us insight or instruction, where He can gently correct and chasten, where He can bring deep healing to a wound that had been previously untouchable. It is anesthesia for the soul. People who work with children know well this technique. As children respond to humor, they become teachable. As children of God are touched by God's anointing oil of joy and experience new depths of laughter and celebration, they become vulnerable to deeper, more powerful works of God in their lives.

> "Humor is a prelude to faith,
> and laughter is the beginning of prayer."
> —*Theologian Reinhold Niebuhr*

Spiritual Connection – Celebrating the Lord of the Dance

Jesus' life capsulizes this teaching on joy. Christ's birth was *good news of great joy that will be for all the people* (Luke 2:10). Even His presence in Mary's womb caused John the Baptist (also still in utero) to leap for joy (Luke 1:44).

Jesus taught that the kingdom of heaven was like a treasure hidden in a field – a treasure worth selling everything for because of the joy it brought (Matthew 13:44-46). Jesus warned His disciples that they would grieve because of His death and parting, but that soon their grieving would turn to joy (John 16:22). In Hebrews, it reads, *Let us fix our eyes on Jesus, the author and perfecter of our faith, who for the joy set before Him endured the cross, scorning its shame, and sat down at the right hand of the throne of God* (Heb. 12:2).

Christ's resurrection is the ultimate source of joy – from death to life! The Son of God, our Savior, who took on our sins and was put to death for them, was laid in a tomb on Friday. But that's not the end of the story. On Sunday, the tomb was empty! And it is still empty! Jesus is alive! This was the ultimate practical joke on Satan, but a miraculous surprise for mankind. Because of His defeat of sin and death, we have hope. Things are not always what they seem. We have joy. We can laugh. We can celebrate.

Practical Applications

Though joy is not something we can manufacture, we can take childlike steps to be in a place where God can produce joy in us. Here is a summary of some of the ideas from this chapter:

1. **Pray.** The first step is to ask God to restore our joy. *Restore to me the joy of your salvation and grant me a willing spirit, to sustain me* (Psalm 51:12). Ask the Lord to anoint you again with the oil of joy. I think we can get even more specific. When I laugh, I tend to laugh silently, which feels restricted and controlled. I am asking the Lord to bring freedom to my

laughter, that it might involve my whole body, that I not be held back from fully expressing the joy that is within. A corollary prayer is for the Lord to help me not take life so seriously.

2. **Be generous.** Don't hold on so tightly to things which can often lead to stress and misery. Learn to be a hilarious giver.

3. **Expose yourself to clean sources of humor.** What really makes you laugh out loud? Make a list and start getting a regular diet of it.

4. **Share all your emotions.** Life is often hard. When we have strong negative emotions and stuff them inside, they act like a deep-seated infection that turns into a boil. Vent to God. Vent to a close friend. Keep a journal.

5. **Make holidays special.** Do something meaningful next time a holiday rolls around. Better yet, don't wait for the holiday. Make the next weekend special. Even celebrating an offbeat holiday like April Fool's Day can become a fun family tradition. My daughter Sarah takes April First very seriously. One year, when she realized on March 31 that the next day was April Fool's Day and she wasn't prepared said, "Oh no, and I don't have any pranks planned. How irresponsible of me!"

6. **Experience the gift of music.** This could be as simple as listening to a favorite composer or artist at home or traveling to a big city to attend an opera or concert. If you have musical abilities, explore how you might use them. My wife and I are taking ballroom

dancing lessons which not only gives us time together but the benefits of exercise and exposure to music as well.

7. **Enjoy God's presence.** Don't limit your time with God to Sunday mornings. Consider attending other church meetings during the week. Make worship a part of your family life together. Learn to rest in God's presence throughout the day. Joy will follow.

Recommended Reading

Foster, Richard. *Celebration of Discipline.* San Francisco: Harper & Row, 1978.

Smith, Hannah Whitall. *A Christian's Secret of A Happy Life.* Whitaker House, 1983.

> "I don't think of all the misery,
> but of the beauty that still remains...
> my advice is: Go outside, to the fields,
> enjoy nature and the sunshine,
> go out and try to recapture
> happiness in yourself and God.
> Think of all the beauty
> that's still left in and around you
> and be happy."
> —*Anne Frank*

SUMMARY

Getting Started on Temple Maintenance

Back when I was in high school, I decided to plant an organic garden. I must have hatched this idea in early June because temperatures in the San Joaquin Valley were already in the 90s. But I plowed ahead anyway, choosing a site alongside the house because it was fenced and the dog couldn't dig there.

Yes, there were little problems with the site. Like the fact that my garden received direct sunlight only between 11 a.m. and 4 p.m. (the hottest part of the day). The other obvious problem was that it was smothered with black plastic and tons of river rock. Because of that, I hadn't bothered to test the soil. If I had, I would have discovered that just under the surface was a layer of thick, hard clay. But no problem. I was absolutely confident that I could soften it up by soaking it with a garden hose.

I drenched it for hours but, to my dismay, only the top half-inch of soil softened up (the clay remained as hard as concrete). But no matter. I pressed on to plant my first crop – two neat rows of carrots. I wanted to keep it simple so that's all I planted (probably the only wise thing I did). When the seeds were in, I stood up and surveyed my work with glowing pride.

> "...You are God's field, God's building."
> —*1 Corinthians 3:9*

For the first week, I watered every other day. Then I grew busy hanging out with friends. About every three or four days I would remember, with a twinge of guilt, my neglect of the garden. Then I would rush out, give it a good soak and hope for the best. When the first green shoots appeared, I was buoyed with encouragement and began to water more consistently. But soon I was back in my old pattern, forgetting to water for days at a time. After one particularly long period of neglect, I hurried out to see if my garden was OK. I hoped to harvest some mature carrots, but instead found dry and dying plants with anemic-looking roots.

That was my first and last gardening experience. Despite the disastrous results, the experience taught me several key principles that can also relate to building and maintaining physical health through rest, diet, exercise, stress management, celebration and other disciplines. Here are some things to consider as you are planting for the future:

Choose the Right Time to Begin

There's a right time to plant a garden. In early spring, the cooler temperatures are less harsh to the younger plants, and it gives them a greater chance to establish themselves. In the Bible we see another example of timing. In a letter to King Hiram, Solomon explains why he – and not his father – was building the temple: *You know that because of the wars waged against my father David from all sides, he could not build a temple for the Name of the Lord his God until the Lord put his enemies under his feet* (1 Kings 5:3). David wanted to build the temple, but he was busy waging wars and subduing enemies. The Lord made it clear to David that his son Solomon was to do this work (2 Samuel 7).

As you make plans to "rebuild your body temple," ask the Lord, "Is this the right time?" Perhaps you are in the midst of a spiritual battle – you are dealing with the enemy related to a struggle with sin, or you are overwhelmed with depression or the recent death of a family member or friend. Don't set yourself up for failure by adding these physical health principles to your already very full plate. Wait for the Lord to release you to pursue these.

> "Dig a well before you are thirsty."
> —*Chinese proverb*

On the other hand, don't use this as a cop-out. You may convince yourself there is never a good time. There is always going to be some stress and turmoil in your life. Perhaps some of the turmoil is a signal that you really need to begin the work. The longer you wait, the longer it will take you to regain your health.

Count the Cost

It would be foolish to plant a garden and then leave on

vacation. A healthy garden requires regular attention. The same is true for starting a program of healthy eating, exercise or rest. It takes effort to establish major lifestyle changes, and you are wise to count the cost before you begin.

In Chapter 5, we mentioned the costs associated with self-control. These same costs apply to the efforts needed to build and maintain a preventive health program. It takes *sacrifice* – a willingness to pay whatever it costs to pursue these principles. It takes *delayed gratification* – a maturity evidenced by a willingness to endure pain and sacrifice now for later rewards. And it takes *discipline* – a character trait best exemplified in the life of Jesus. But above these is the cost of taking *responsibility*.

When Solomon saw that the time was right for starting the temple, he began the project by taking responsibility. *I intend, therefore, to build a temple...* (1 Kings 5:5). He made a decision and took responsibility for carrying it out.

In every building program someone has to be ultimately responsible, and in the building up of your body-temple, that person is you (not your spouse, your doctor or even God). I see patients every day who are suffering the direct results of poor lifestyle choices but won't take responsibility for their health. Their body is like their automobile. When it breaks down or malfunctions, they want it fixed immediately but refuse to follow the manufacturer's maintenance guidelines. They are running their engine nonstop. They are going over the speed limit or over bumpy roads, causing stress and strain on their system. They are using low octane fuel, allowing the battery to run low on water, and using a dirty air filter. They are driving without insurance and only to work, never to play.

> "Our doubts are traitors, and make us lose the good we oft might gain by fearing to attempt."
> —*Shakespeare*

They won't regain the health they want until they accept responsibility. If you are one of these people, I urge you to take this first step. The Lord will help you. He is ready to assist and guide you to a healthier life, and you have to do your part.

Get Your Motives Right

When I planted the carrots in that patch of hard earth next to my bedroom window, my motivation was certainly suspect. I probably thought, "Hey, having an organic garden is going to be fun and easy." Actually, it wasn't as much fun as I thought it might be, and it was easier to go to the health food store and buy the carrots. Without a strong enough motive, we will likely fail at whatever health disciplines we initiate.

In 1 Kings 5:5, Solomon declared, *I intend, therefore, to build a temple for the Name of the Lord my God....* That purpose kept him focused through all the hard work and expense. The temple was to be a reminder to the people of God's presence among them. What better motivation could there be to make the temple beautiful, excellent and glorious?

Likewise, the highest possible motive for rebuilding our body-temples is so they may bring glory to God and be fit for serving him. God, the Holy Spirit, lives within us. He is our invited guest, and this guest deserves the best habitation that we can provide. The lifestyle choices we make and the actions we take tell God and others whether we love or hate our body-temples (Eph. 5:29). What is the message you are broadcasting to the world?

One of God's most effective tools for helping us change is our imagination. Somehow, in our twentieth century analytical mindset, we have discarded the power of imagination as either childish, ineffective or connected with New Age thinking. Yet what is faith and hope without a vision of what God can do? That's why Paul calls us to set our minds on things above and to think about things that are true, noble, right, pure, lovely, admirable, excellent and praiseworthy (Col. 3:2, Phil. 4:8). Because Paul saw through eyes of faith, he could declare (and we can echo him), *I can do all things through Christ who strengthens me* (Phil. 4:13 NKJV).

As we imagine ourselves fit and healthy, we are actually offering up a prayer of faith and hope to God. We are seeing what he desires.

Get Help From Others

One of the big mistakes I made with my garden was trying to do it alone. This, of course, is one of the health principles we discussed earlier. We need each other. There are plenty of resources for someone wanting to start a garden. There are books to buy or borrow. There are plenty of experts – gardeners, nursery workers and horticulturists you can turn to. There are classes you might take and information on the Internet.

Solomon showed greater wisdom with his building project. He asked for help from Hiram, king of Tyre. He got some experts involved because he had *no one so skilled in felling timber as the Sidonians* (1 Kings 5:6). He also found an expert artisan for the temple furnishings – a man called Huram – who was skilled in bronze work.

Your body-temple rebuilding project deserves a network of support as well. If you have a personal physician, go to him (or her) and discuss your plans. Especially if you are on medication for a chronic condition, you need to discuss with your doctor what kind of dietary and exercise changes you plan to start. Get advice about how quickly to progress in these lifestyle changes and ask if he or she will help to monitor you. Most physicians are thrilled to assist patients interested in making these changes. If they are skeptical or unsupportive, then consider finding a physician who will help.

The fact you are reading this book (and have made it this far) indicates you are serious about improving your physical health. Don't stop reading. Search out the Word of God for yourself and see what truths you find. Explore some of the recommended resources at the end of each chapter.

> "We must never get too busy sawing
> to take time to sharpen the saw,
> never too busy driving
> to take time to get gas."
> —*Stephen R. Covey*

Aim for Prevention

While I was in medical school, a pediatrician gave a lecture that prompted my thinking about routine well-child care. He noted that the American Academy of Pediatrics recommends every child to see a pediatrician at ages 2, 4, 6, 9, 12, 15, 18 and 24 months. When I first heard this, I assumed that the AAP recommended that many visits so doctors could make more money. Later on, I changed my thinking. The first two years of life are critical. An infant's body is changing rapidly and growth is occurring at a phenomenal rate – more than at any other time in a person's life. By having frequent check-ups, guidance counseling can occur, developmental milestones can be monitored, a growth chart can be plotted, and immunizations can be given. Problems can often be avoided or detected early, so treatment is more effective. People need a healthy start in life, and well-child checkups provide true preventive care.

If we took these principles into childhood, adolescence and young adulthood, and actually taught kids God's principles of health, think of the impact it would have on medical care and on the church! However, today when I see an adult in my office, most insurance companies will not cover such things as "preventive care counseling" or a "nutritional assessment." By contrast, the dental profession has switched its focus from "drilling and filling" to preventive care, and our dental health has improved significantly.

Personalizing Your Health Program

Even if you're not experiencing major health problems right now, you are wise to consider implementing measures of preventive care. In fact, this is an ideal time to make changes – before major health issues arise. But where do you start? It can seem overwhelming to even think about major lifestyle changes. Let me suggest you do some soul-searching and praying on this one. It is not going to be the same for everyone. Here are some considerations:

1. Begin with rest – As mentioned in Chapter 1, I believe the beginning point is rest. We need adequate sleep.

We need to establish a regular cycle of Sabbath. And we need occasional times of retreat, lasting from one to three days. Before you pursue any other changes, I strongly suggest that you learn how to receive God's rest.

2. Decide on your top priority – Often the Lord puts desires in our hearts, and we need to listen to these. You might feel a need to start fasting regularly. Begin there. Maybe you are interested in healthier eating and are "ripe" for a change. Go for it. Perhaps you have felt a need to begin an exercise program. Listen to these nudges from the Lord. If we follow the Lord's leading, our chances of success are much greater. If you don't have a clear leading on priorities, take time with the Lord to ask for His priorities for you.

3. Look into the stress factor – If stress or anxiety are obvious problems in your life, make this one of your top priorities. As mentioned in Chapter 2, anxiety can affect all aspects of health. When this is not dealt with, it can be very difficult to start a new diet, quit smoking or make other lifestyle changes.

To release your stress: Get a counselor. Get into God's Word. Find positive outlets. Praise. Confess. Meditate. Of course, exercise is an excellent outlet for stress, and should be pursued simultaneously. Because of their interconnectedness, it is difficult to practice only one of these health principles in isolation. On the other hand, most people have trouble incorporating the whole package at once. (See more about this below.)

4. Establish support early-on – You need accountability. You need encouragement. You need to know you're not alone. Find others who are interested in improving their physical health. Do your building together.

5. Begin with small steps – Crown Ministries teaches us to list all our debts and to begin paying on the smallest debt until it is paid off. Then use the entire amount you were paying on that debt and apply it to the next smallest debt until it is paid off. Continue the process until all the debts are paid off. This is encouraging because each victory builds toward the next.

The same principle can be applied here. What would you consider a small step toward better health? Maybe it would be to drink 64 ounces of water a day. Don't try to stop the negative at first (the four sodas a day), but instead just add the positive. Maybe a small step would be to fast for 12 hours once a week. Maybe it would be to walk five minutes everyday. Maybe it would be to join a support group. Maybe it would be to eat five servings of fruits and vegetables. After you have accomplished this small step and consistently practiced it for four to six weeks, then consider adding another small step to what you are already doing. Now instead of five minutes, your goal might be to walk ten minutes. Besides the servings of fruits and vegetables, you add the goal of two meatless meals each week. Continue to keep your long-term goal in mind, but rejoice when baby steps are taken.

6. Celebrate small victories – As you incorporate a small step into your lifestyle, set up specific times and ways to celebrate your victories. These can be large or small celebrations depending on the circumstances. Generally, it is a good idea for the celebration to be health-promoting. Going out for pepperoni pizza in celebration of a positive change in diet is somewhat self-defeating. Consider going to a restaurant with healthier choices instead. Go to the park with your family or a friend. Go to a movie. Spend an hour playing a computer game. The idea is to find something you enjoy within your budget that you normally don't get to do.

7. Exercise early – Begin an exercise program early in your program, if possible. The rewards of regular exercise appear quickly compared with some of the other health habits. And exercise affects several of the other habits. It can help us sleep better. It can be a great stress reliever. It can help digestion. It can teach us about self-control. It can be an activity that includes fellowship and helps us connect with people. The increased energy you feel shortly after starting an exercise program can be directed toward one or more of the other health habits.

8. Schedule maintenance into your day – Many times people need help in remembering to do the health habits – until they become second nature. I use my daily planner to help. When I am planning my week, I write down on specific days whether I will be doing aerobic or strengthening exercises. For every day I write four W's. I use a 16-ounce cup and fill it with water. I drink one cup before breakfast, one cup before lunch, one before dinner and one before bedtime. Each time I drink a cup, I check off one of the W's in my planner.

I don't need to do that for Sabbath. It is an established habit in my life that Sunday is set aside to be a Sabbath rest. If I am on call or involved in something else on a Sunday, I try to schedule the Sabbath time on another day that week.

I also use the planner for scheduling times when I plan to fast. If I don't plan ahead, I tend to neglect this habit. I do the same thing for scheduling times of personal retreat. Just as someone may need to schedule prayer and quiet time with the Lord in order to be consistent, so we often need to schedule the physical health disciplines. This is not intended to be a law that kills, but a tool to bring life.

> "No discipline seems pleasant at the time, but painful. Later on, however, it produces a harvest of righteousness and peace for those who have been trained by it."
> —*Hebrews 12:11*

9. Review your progress periodically – It is helpful to regularly step back and take inventory of your physical health. If you have written down health goals for yourself for one month, three months, six months, one year, five years and ten years, then when those times come, take time to review what you have accomplished. Make adjustments. Reevaluate your priorities. Ask the Lord how you are doing. Ask yourself the same question. Ask your doctor. Record the changes you have seen in a journal. Reread this book.

10. Consider (with caution) a more rapid approach – Incorporating even one of these health principles into your life can be an overwhelming goal. So making several lifestyle changes at once can be a setup for failure. Yet there may be times when someone is called by God to move through this process more rapidly than normally recommended. To do this with success, these are what I believe are minimum requirements:

- A clear directive from God to move more quickly in this process.
- A written statement of your primary motives (use your imagination to form your vision).
- A commitment of support from friends, family or a regular support group.
- A willingness to return to a slower approach if the more rapid one is too overwhelming.

Our Body-Temple – a Picture of Our Relationship with God?

From the time Solomon built it until the Babylonians set fire to it over 360 years later, the temple was a constant reminder to the Israelites of their relationship to Jehovah God. It was also a reflection of their spiritual condition. The temple's condition spoke to anyone passing by about whether Israel was more interested in worshipping God or serving themselves. The desecration of the temple in Jerusalem actually started with Solomon himself. He took many foreign wives and built for them "high places" where they could sacrifice to their gods. His son Rehoboam took it a step further, setting up Asherah poles on every high hill and even allowing male shrine prostitution. Rehoboam's weak and spiritually corrupt kingdom emboldened Egypt to attack Jerusalem and loot the temple of its treasures.

Over the next 100 years there were some good kings and some evil kings, but the temple was generally neglected by all. It was in need of significant repairs when Joash became king, and he orchestrated these repairs through money collected from the people. One of the lowest points in the temple's history was when Manasseh became king of Judah. He rebuilt the high places his father Hezekiah had destroyed. He built altars in the temple dedicated to the stars and even sacrificed his own son on one of them. He practiced sorcery and divination, and consulted mediums and spiritists.

When Manasseh's grandson Josiah became king, the temple was in horrible disrepair. The spiritual condition of the nation was so bad that the Book of the Law had been lost and nobody even knew it until Josiah ordered repairs on the temple. When the priests found the book and started reading it, they were struck to the heart over their neglect of God's Word. This sparked a remarkable cleansing of the nation as Josiah removed any trace of the pagan practices and reestablished the Passover Feast.

These steps were significant for that generation, but too late to incur a lasting change in the lives and hearts of the people. The next four kings returned to the evil practices of their forefathers, and only 25 years after Josiah's death, the Babylonians orchestrated the fall of Jerusalem.

> *God handed all of them over to Nebuchadnezzar. He carried to Babylon all the articles from the temple of God, both large and small, and the treasures of the Lord's temple and the treasures of the king and his officials. They set fire to God's temple and broke down the wall of Jerusalem; they burned all the palaces and destroyed everything of value there* (2 Chron. 36:17-19).

The destruction of the temple and the captivity of the Israelites could have been avoided. By following God's laws, the people's health and freedom, and the integrity of the temple would have endured. The good news was that God met them where they were and eventually led them back into His long-range plans. The bad news was the temporary suffering and devastation as the people were focused primarily on their misery and loss, instead of partnering with God with joy and purpose.

My prayer is that you have heard a gentle nudge from the Lord to begin to repair His temple. It is time to honor our bodies by dedicating them to Him and following His rebuilding program. Many of us have neglected our temples long enough.

Let us each take the hand of our God and allow Him to lead us to more abundant health – spiritually, emotionally and physically. The choices are before us, and God graciously invites us to choose life and blessing. Come!

Recommended Reading

Omartian, Stormie. *Greater Health God's Way*. Eugene: Harvest House, 1996.

McMillen, M.D., S.I., revised and updated by David E. Stern, M.D. *None of These Diseases*. Grand Rapids: Revell, 1963, 1984.

A workbook is being developed to complement this book. If you are interested in ordering a workbook, additional books or giving comments, you may do so through the email address: rkleyn@lightspeed.net.

APPENDIX 1

God's Attributes

1. *God Is* – In the beginning God (Gen. 1:1); "I AM WHO I AM." (Exod. 3:14).

2. *God is Living* – He is not an inanimate idol, but the living, active God (Jer. 10:5,10).

3. *God is Personal* – He has personal names and relationships with people (Num. 12:8; Lev. 26:12).

4. *God is Spirit* – His worshipers must worship in spirit and in truth (John 4:24).

5. *God is Transcendent* – He is the Lord "high and lifted up" (Isa. 6:1).

6. *God is Incomprehensible Yet Knowable* – His ways and thoughts are higher than ours (Isa. 55:9); We can

know Him deeply (Jer. 9:24).

7. *God is Love* – His love is unfathomable. Nothing can separate us from it (Eph. 3:17-19; Rom. 8:35-39).

8. *God is Sovereign* – He is in control and will reign forever (1 Chron. 29:11; Ex. 15:18). He knows every creature (Ps. 50:10,11); He determines times and places (Acts 17:24-26).

9. *God is Eternal and Infinite* – He's from everlasting to everlasting (Ps. 90:2) and not confined (Job 11:7-9).

10. *God is Immutable (Unchanging)* – He is the Rock (2 Sam. 22:47); He's always the same (Heb. 13:8).

11. *God is Omnipotent* – Nothing is too hard for the God of miracles (Jer. 32:17; Ps. 77:14).

12. *God is Omnipresent* – He fills heaven and earth (Jer. 23:24); you can't escape His presence (Ps. 139:7-12).

13. *God is Omniscient* – He knows us completely; He knows the future (Ps. 139; 1 John 3:20; Heb. 4:13).

14. *God is Wisdom* – His wisdom is seen in creation, displayed through history, and ultimately demonstrated in the cross of Christ (Ps. 104:24; Dan. 2:20-22; 1 Cor. 1:20-25).

15. *God is Faithful* – Great is His faithfulness (Lam. 3:23; Deut. 7:9; 1 John 1:9).

16. *God is Holy* – He is majestic in holiness (Exod. 15:11; 1 Chron. 16:29).

17. *God is Righteous and Just* – He's righteous in all His ways (Ps. 145:17); His ways are just (Deut. 32:4).

18. *God is Our Father* – He allows us to call Him 'Abba' or 'Daddy' (Gal. 4:6); He disciplines His children (Heb. 12:7).

19. *God is Merciful and Gracious* – He does not treat us as our sins deserve (Ps. 103:10); His grace is sufficient (2 Cor. 12:9); we are saved by His grace (Eph. 2:8).

20. *God is Forgiving* – God forgives wickedness, rebellion, and sin (Exod. 34:6,7); He forgives and forgets (Isa. 43:25); offered through faith in Jesus (Acts 10:43).

21. *God is Good* – In everything, God works for good in those who love Him (Rom. 8:28; Ps. 118:1).

22. *God is Truth* – God is the "living and true God" (1 Thess. 1:9); the word of the Lord is true (John 17:17).

23. *God is Glorious* – His glory is revealed in creation (Ps. 19); His glory is revealed in Jesus (John 1:14).

24. *God is Our Righteousness* – Jehovah-tsidkenu (1 Cor. 1:30; Rom. 3:22-26).

25. *God is Our Sanctifier*- Jehovah-M'Kaddesh (Micah 7:7-11; Heb. 10:10).

26. *God is Our Peace* – Jehovah-shalom (Isa. 54:10; Phil. 4:7).

27. *God is Our Healer* – Jehovah-rophe (Isa. 53:5; Matt. 8:17).

28. *God is Our Provider* – Jehovah-jireh (Isa. 54:1-5; Gen. 22:8).

29. *God is Our Banner* – Jehovah-nissi (Isa. 49:8-26; 1 Cor. 15:57; 2 Cor. 2:14).

30. *God is Our Shepherd* – Jehovah-rohi (Ps. 23; John 10:11).

31. *God is There* – Jehovah-shammah (Isa. 49:14-16; 1 Cor. 3:16).

Adapted from *To Know Him Is to Love and Praise Him! A Bible Study of God's Attributes*, by Beverly Doswald, 1988.

APPENDIX 2

Who Am I?

1. I am the salt of the earth (Matt. 5:13).
2. I am the light of the world (Matt. 5:14).
3. I am part of the true vine, a channel of Christ's life (John 15:1,5).
4. I am Christ's friend (John 15:15).
5. I am chosen and appointed by Christ to bear His fruit (John 15:16).
6. I am a slave of righteousness (Rom 6:18); enslaved to God (Rom. 6:22).
7. I am a son of God; God is spiritually my Father (Rom. 8:14,15; Gal. 3:26;4:6).
8. I am a joint heir with Christ, sharing His inheritance

with Him (Rom. 8:17).

9. I am a temple of the Holy Spirit who dwells in me (1 Cor. 3:16; 6:19).
10. I am united to the Lord and am one spirit with Him (1 Cor. 6:17).
11. I am a member of Christ's body (1 Cor. 12:17; Eph. 5:30).
12. I am a new creation (2 Cor. 5:17).
13. I am reconciled to God and am a minister of reconciliation (2 Cor. 5:18,19).
14. I am a saint (Eph. 1:1; 1 Cor. 1:2; Phil. 1:1; Col. 1:2).
15. I am God's workmanship born anew in Christ to do His work (Eph. 2:10).
16. I am a fellow citizen with the rest of God's family (Eph. 2:19).
17. I am a prisoner of Christ (Eph. 3:1; 4:1).
18. I am righteous and holy (Eph. 4:24).
19. I am a citizen of heaven, seated in heaven right now (Phil. 3:20; Eph. 2:6).
20. I am hidden with Christ in God (Col. 3:3).
21. I am an expression of the life of Christ because He is my life (Col. 3:4).
22. I am chosen of God, holy and dearly loved (Col. 3:12; 1 Thess. 1:4).
23. I am a son of light and not of darkness (1 Thess. 5:5).
24. I am a holy partaker of a heavenly calling (Heb. 3:1).

25. I am a partaker of Christ; I share in His life (Heb. 3:14).
26. I am one of God's living stones, being built up in Christ as a spiritual house (1 Pet. 2:5).
27. I am a member of a chosen race, a royal priesthood, a holy nation (1 Pet. 2:9,10).
28. I am an alien and stranger to this world in which I temporarily live (1 Pet. 2:11).
29. I am an enemy of the devil (1 Pet. 5:8).
30. I am a child of God and I will resemble Christ when He returns (1 John 3:2).
31. I am not the great "I am" (Exod. 3:14; John 8:24,28,58), but by God's grace, I am what I am (1 Cor. 15:10).

Adapted from: *Victory Over the Darkness*; Neil T. Anderson. Regal Books, 1990, pp. 45-47.

ENDNOTES

◆

[1] Ezra 5:17; 6:12.

[2] Tim Hansel, *When I Relax I Feel Guilty* (Chariot Family Publishers, 1984) p. 35.

[3] Marva J. Dawn, *Keeping the Sabbath Wholly* (Grand Rapids: William B. Eerdmans Publishing Co., 1989) p. xi.

[4] Ibid, p. 6,7.

[5] I also hightly recommend the simple, practical and effective guidelines described in the book, *Listening Prayer*, by Dave and Linda Olson. Available by calling 1-935-447-9458 (El Cajon, CA).

[6] Mayer has adapted this from a technique described by Herbert Benson, M.D., in his book, *Timeless Healing* (New York: Simon & Schuster, 1996).

[7] "Faith Can Help You Heal," *Reader's Digest*, October 1998, p. 111.

[8] Archibald D. Hart, *Adrenalin and Stress* (Dallas: Word Publishing, 1986) p. 67.

[9] Published in *Biofeedback and Self-Regulation*, Vol. 7, No. 1, 1982.

[10] Richard A. Swenson, M.D., *Margin: Restoring Emotional, Physical, Financial, and Time Reserves to Overloaded Lives* (Colorado Springs: Navpress, 1992) p. 67.

[11] Drs. Dan B. Allender & Tremper Longman III, *The Cry of the Soul* (Colorado Springs: Navpress, 1994) p. 99.

[12] Susan Jeffers, Ph.D., *Feel the Fear and Do It Anyway* (New York: Fawcett Columbine, 1987) p. 22.

[13] Allender & Longman, p. 104.

[14] Based on a sermon by Pastor Brad Davis.

[15] Jeffers, p. 30.

[16] Adapted from a sermon by the late Rev. Roy Hicks Jr., Faith Center, Eugene OR.

[17] One good resource is *Discovering the Enneagram*, by Richard Rohr (New York: Crossroad, 1990).

[18] John McDougall, MD, *The McDougall Plan* (New Win Publishing, 1983) pp. 76-94.

[19] O. Schell, *Modern Meat* (Vintage Books, 1985).

[20] Comptroller General's Report, *Problems of Preventing the Marketing of Raw Meat and Poultry Containing Harmful Residues*, Government Documents Collection, GA 1.13, HRD 79-10.

[21] Irving Fisher, "The Influence of Flesh Eating on Endurance," *Yale Medical Journal*, 13 (5):205-221.

[22] Per-Olaf Astrand, *Nutrition Today*, 3: No. 2, 9-11, 1968.

[23] McDougall, p. 15.

[24] *Ibid*, p. 7.

[25] Data obtained from "Nutritive Value of American Foods in Common Units," *USDA Handbook*, No. 456.

[26] R. Mazess, "Bone Mineral Content of North Alaskan Eskimos," *American Journal of Clinical Nutrition*, 27 (1974):916.

[27] A. Walker, "Osteoporosis and Calcium Deficiency," *American Journal of Clinical Nutrition*, 16 (1965):327.

[28] T.C. Campbell, quoted in Lang's "Diet and Disease," *Food Monitor*, May/June 1983, p. 24.

[29] T. Osborn, "Amino Acids in Nutrition and Growth," *Journal of Biological Chemistry*, 17 (1914):325.

[30] W. Rose, "Comparative Growth of Diets Containing Ten and Nineteen Amino Acids," *Journal of Biological Chemistry*, 176 (1948):753.

[31] W. Rose, "The Amino Acid Requirements of Adult Men," *Nutritional Abstracts and Reviews*, 27 (1957):631.

[32] George Malkmus, *God's Way to Ultimate Health* (Eidson: Hallelujah Acres Publ., 1995) p. 129.

[33] McDougall, p. 55.

[34] Ibid, pp. 52,53.

[35] John McDougall, MD, "Salt's PL?" *The McDougall Newsletter*, July-Aug. 1996, p. 5.

[36] R. Phillips, "Coronary heart disease mortality among Seventh Day Adventists with differing dietary habits," Abstract American Public Health Association Meeting, Chicago, Nov. 16-20 1975.

[37] McDougall, *The McDougall Plan*, p. 85.

[38] John Robbins, *Diet for a New America* (Walpole: Stillpoint Publishing, 1987) p. 277.

[39] B. Reddy, "Nutrition and its relationship to cancer," *Advances in Cancer Research*, 32:327, 1980.

[40] Mayer and Goldberg, Nutrition (syndicated column), *Washington Post*, July 26, 1981.

[41] James F. Balch, M.D. and Phyllis A. Balch, C.N.C., *Prescription for Nutritional Healing* (Avery Publishing Group) p. 547.

[42] S.N. Blair, H.W. Kohl, R.S. Paffenbarger, et al, "Physical fitness and all-cause mortality," *Journal of American Medical Association*, 1989; 262:2395-2401.

[43] A.S. Leon, J. Connett, D.R. Jacobs, et al, "Leisure-time physical activity levels and risk of heart disease and death. The multiple risk factor intervention trial," *Journal of American Medical Association*, 1987; 258:2388-95.

[44] Dean Ornish, M.D., *Dr. Dean Ornish's Program for Reversing Heart Disease* (New York: Ballantine Books, 1990) p. 326.

[45] Larsen and Hegarty, *Days of Healing, Days of Joy* (New York: Harper/Hazelden, 1987).

[46] James C. Thompson, "Seed Corn," *Biomedical Inquiry*, Fall 1996, p. 2.

[47] Stormie Omartian, *Greater Health God's Way* (Eugene: Harvest House Publishers, 1996) p. 255.

[48] Anthony de Mello, *Taking Flight: A Book of Story Meditations* (New York: Doubleday, 1988) pp. 114-115.

[49] John & Paula Sandford, *Restoring the Christian Family* (Tulsa: Victory House, 1979) p. 168.

[50] Based on the work of John & Paula Sandford, *Healing the Wounded Spirit* (Tulsa: Victory House, 1985) Chapter 5, "The Slumbering Spirit," pp. 105-144.

[51] Brennan Manning, *The Ragamuffin Gospel* (Sisters: Multnomah Publishers, 1990) pp. 46, 47. Emphasis added.

[52] Larry Briney, "Cause and Effect!" Valley Christian Center bulletin, Feb. 22, 1987.

[53] Frank Minirth, *Love Hunger: Recovery from Food Addiction* (Fawcett, May 1991).

[54] *The 12 Steps: A Way Out* (Recovery Publications, Sept. 1995).

[55] David Spiegel, "Effect of Psychosocial Treatments on Survival of Patients with Metastatic Breast Cancer," *The Lancet*, 2 (8668): 888-91, 1989, Oct. 14.

[56] Berkman and Syme, "Social networks, host resistance, and mortality: a nine year follow up study of Alameda County residents," *American Journal of Epidemiology,* 1979; 109(2):186-204. Kaplan, Salonen, Cohen, Brand et al, "Social connections and mortality from all causes and from cardiovascular disease: prospective evidence from eastern Finland," *American Journal of Epidemiology,* 1988; 128(2):370-80.

57 House, Landis and Umberson, "Social relationships and health," *Science,* 1988; 241(4865):540-45.

58 Stu Weber, "Some One to Lean On," *Focus on the Family,* June 1996, p. 2.

59 Richard Foster, *Celebration of Discipline* (New York: Harper & Row, 1978) pp. 159-160.

60 Alan McGinnis, *The Friendship Factor* (Minneapolis: Augsberg Publishing , 1979) p. 85.

61 Ibid., p. 91.

62 Foster, pp. 159-160.

63 Norman Cousins, *Anatomy of an Illness* (New York: W.W. Norton, 1979).

64 Lee Berk, "Neuroendocrine and stress hormone changes during mirthful laughter,"*American Journal of Medical Sciences.* 1989; 298:390-396.

65 Mary Roach, "The Power of Laughter," *Hippocrates,* Jan. 1997, 47-50.

66 Ibid.

67 Foster, p. 168.

68 Tom Mullen, *Seriously, Life Is a Laughing Matter* (Waco: Word Books, 1978) p. 32.

69 Foster, Ibid, p. 167.

70 *Website of the American Assn. of Therapeutic Humor:* http://www.ideanurse.comaath/

71 The first two jokes are attributed to Henny Youngman; source of the third is unknown.

72 Foster, Ibid, p. 167.